MW01167031

07/ 18/ 05

Thank you.

OCEAN OF BLUE TEARS

A WORLD OF THE UNTOLD

BY

PRINCE A GORDON

1663 LIBERTY DRIVE, SUITE 200
BLOOMINGTON, INDIANA 47403
(800) 839-8640
WWW.AUTHORHOUSE.COM

First published by AuthorHouse 01/18/05

ISBN: 1-4184-6094-X (e)
ISBN: 1-4184-6095-8 (sc)

Library of Congress Control Number: 2004095433

Printed in the United States of America
Bloomington, Indiana

This book is printed on acid-free paper.

Introduction

The pathway I chose to travel during this time was a dark and rocky one; still, I was blinded to what the future held in store for me. This pathway caused me to experience the worst side of human dignity, a side of man that protested against equality and human relation, a side of man that rejected the opposite sex, a side that rejected the embracing side of wisdom, a side of self-conceit. What I have experienced there was more than the capacity of deeper things. I have worked on four different cruise lines, and their systems were one-sided and alike. I have taken great pleasure in using this privilege to share with you my twelve years' experience as a seaman. I can assure you with the greatest respect that where misleading is concerned I am not ignorant My personal and true experience will carefully guide you through a world of the untold and the unknown. I must truly say that the content of this book has nothing to do with racism, religion, nationality, or culture. The content of this book is not based on revenge, hate, rage, or intended to disgrace. I have seen human lives become human waste. I have seen plots to kill. I have seen the dead walk. I have seen disregard for the perishing. I have looked behind the flesh of man with only true guidance and recognized that the souls of those who were crippled were affected by excessive and evil sources of drugs. I did believe that entering a different world's civilization would offer me an equal opportunity to earning. I have recognized with true guidance that partiality and hate sit in the laps of fools. Corruption and abomination are a condemnation to he who gives life and true wisdom. For all the evil deeds that I experienced, still my heart was filled with love and forgiveness.

Chapter-1

In the early eighties, I signed a contract for one year with a certain cruise line that was based in the United States. This company was well known and recognized because they had been in this operation for several years. This cruise line sailed all over the Caribbean and the Pacific Ocean. For a passenger line, they were well kept and recommended and like any other line that I worked with. If you had been on one, you had been on all. For a crew from the island, the system worked the same for us as it did for any of the sister ships. Never in my life would I have dreamt that I would spend twelve years of my natural life among people who were mentally sick. I never believed I would work amongst racism, hate, injustice, and discrimination, among thieves, drunkards, murderers, liars, gamblers, drug addicts, gays, and uncivilized people—until I arrived here in the early eighties to fulfill my contract.

When reporting to the main office that afternoon, the first person I confronted was the personnel manager. I handed him all the documents I arrived with. He said, "Sit down, sir. I will be right with you."

It was approximately one hour before he returned because there were other applicants to be processed. After all the paperwork was done, he handed me the address of the company doctor, whom I had to see, along with the other men, to get a physical checkup. We all took taxis to the medical center. The cab driver did not run the meter that day. We thought he cut us a good deal but later learned that he overcharged us when telling us the cost. There were four men to a cab, and some of the men were upset that indecent language was used during the drive.

As we entered the doctor's office, I said good afternoon to the nurse. She was pretty, but I did not lust for her. Other men from different companies were also waiting to be

1

checked. As we handed her the company documents, she gave us a form to fill out before we could see the doctor. I realized that not all the guys there could fill out the forms.

When it was my turn to see the doctor, the nurse called me inside a small room and gave me a chair to sit on. She said, "You look nervous."

"No," I replied.

She ran several tests on me first (hearing test, eye test, blood test, urine test, feces test, chest x-ray) then put me in a room to wait. It was a very quiet room until the doctor entered the room and broke the silence. I wanted to get this exam over with. The only thing that was on my mind was the job. "Hello, Doctor," I said.

"Hello, sir," he answered. He told me to get undressed. I left on my underwear. He turned to me and said, "Everything, sir.", After doing some more tests, everything was going great until he told me to bend over. He pulled on a pair of latex gloves then lubricated one finger, and without another word, the doctor started to feel for a pile. My whole day was spoiled. At least the examination was over. We had to pass our physical exams or else we couldn't work. Those who found it difficult to pass their tests had to return for another appointment.

Later that day, we returned to the main office to surrender our fitness forms. Because the group of us had the whole evening for ourselves, we decided to walk back to the hotel that the company provided for us; it couldn't have been more than one mile. We passed through a small neighborhood. I wasn't looking for any poverty in America, then I saw people sleeping under the overhead roads that I would call back home bridges. I asked why these people were sleeping there. Someone in the group who had traveled before said, "That's his home."

I said with shock, "You are lying." We continued to pass through this little town. I couldn't believe the amount of unemployed people who lived there. We were later told that it was not safe for us strangers to walk through that area, especially at night. We reached the hotel at last, where we would spend two to four days at the company's expense. Those days were the good old days; now the companies draw such expenses from our salaries. The first thing I needed was a cold shower and rest from the long walk back to the hotel.

Chapter-2

Later that evening, I relaxed watching the news channel. I went to the restaurant to have my dinner at eight PM. The restaurant was very small with the capacity of twenty people at one time. The hotel was full because there was more than one company's employees staying there. As the restaurant became full, I waited a good half-hour before I got the chance to eat. It was nothing fancy, just a fast-food restaurant. The old-timers always got served first because they stayed there more than once, and the workers were used to their tips. Finally I was served, without a smile, but that meant nothing to me; I just wanted something to eat. The food was not great. It was kind of tough on my stomach. I had to drink plenty of milk to keep down the grease. Every single crew complained about the food.

The rooms were a total mess with up to six men sharing a room with one shower. It was the first time in my life I shared a room with different nationalities. The bathroom was very nasty. Each man used the basin and the mirror and did not clean it for the next in line. The toilet, when used, was never flushed. Clothing was thrown all over the room. When one man or two broke wind, I had to stay outside the door to breathe fresh air. In order to use a clean shower, I had to visit other rooms that were occupied by other Caribbean men—during the daytime. I never left the room at night because some crewmen's fingers were very light. Plus, thieves from the outside broke in while the crew was out.

The last night in the hotel, every man began to pack his things because the next morning a bus would be escorting us to the ship. I tried not to get myself into any trouble on the last night, so I stayed off the streets and watched television and then fell asleep. The next morning, the phone rang, and I answered it. We were informed that our bus was there to pick us up. Everything was prepacked, so all we did was rush down to catch the bus. I was a little excited on the way as the dock became closer and closer. I could see the ship from a distance. "Here she is!" I shouted to the men. There she was, sitting and waiting to make her next move down to the Caribbean island, where sunshine, green mountains, plantation tours, shopping, and excellent beaches would meet everyone's expectations. The bus driver stopped alongside the ship. We got out, unloaded our luggage, and walked up the gangway. The driver was in front, leading the way to the chief steward's office, where all the new sign-ons would fill out some more forms and receive their cabin keys.

In trying to adjust myself to my new home while searching for my cabin, I got lost because of the many turns. The first person who would notice and try to help you would be a gay man. Some were very friendly and nice. I said, "Hello, can you help me find my cabin please?"

The dear gay man said, "Follow me."

I followed him and found my cabin. "Thank you," I said.

The gay man answered, "You are welcome. Call on me anytime; don't be afraid." These guys were always looking for a new mate when there was a newcomer. Lucky for him, he did not try anything or else I would have fixed his business with a right hand. The true fact was that there were some gays sleeping with each other on board. Some looked, walked, and talked like ladies. I could only try to act antisocial so they would understand that they were barking up the wrong tree.

I pushed the key into my cabin door then opened it. Suddenly, a strong odor hit me in the face. "My God," I said, "something must have died in here." Quickly I stepped back to avoid the odor and let the room blow out before I reentered. This reminded me of the hotel room. I looked at the names posted outside the door and noticed that this cabin was for utility men. "Maybe they are short of waiter cabins," I said to myself.

I went inside and looked around. No one was inside. On the walls, there were pictures of naked girls and pictures of the guys who lived there. At least I knew what they looked like before I met them in person. The only bed inside the cabin that was empty was the top bunk, which meant that it was mine. It was disgusting moving around the sweaty utility uniforms and smelly water booth.

` I tried my best to clean out the cabin and unpacked my clothing. The laundry was not far from my cabin, so I got some fresh linen and made my bed. Then I lay down to rest for a while.

Chapter-3

In the cool of the evening, as the sun was getting ready to take its next descent, the embarkation of the passengers was complete, and all crew members were assumed to be on board. The gangway closed, and all ropes were released. I could hear the engines starting to rumble, and the heavy smoke was released from the chimney. Getting ready for a full night of 18 knots, I was up on deck trying not to miss any of the scenery while she slowly pulled out of port. So many people were waving goodbye to their friends and loved ones. In the meantime, I started to separate myself from the crowd. I ran into the same gay man who helped me earlier. "You lost again?" he asked.

Quickly I answered, "No. Everything is just fine." It was hard for me to believe what was going on here. There were all kinds of crew members on board with different skills. Being next door to them, I could hardly sleep because of the excitement going on, which was very loud.

Anyway, that same evening, I started to study my rules and regulations booklet just to cultivate my mind on the company policy. There were so many rules it was like going back to school again. It was almost time to get ready to go upstairs to see the dining room manager. Nobody told me I would be doing a utility job. First, I would have to take a shower outside my cabin because the ship was old, and all the bathrooms and toilets were outside. To use the toilet, I had to clean it then spread some paper before I could sit. Most of the crew stood on top when using the bowl. To my surprise, there was one gay man who lived right in front of the bathroom door. His door never closed at any time. All he did was lay down on his bed and watch the men going in and out of the bathroom. Me and some other guys who were straight dislike this faggot.

After finishing my shower, I went back to my cabin to get dressed because I had to see the dining room manager. I did not have any appetite that evening, so I bypassed the crew mess. I was still homesick at the time, and it was killing me. I was in my black pants, white shirt, black tie, and black shoes, not knowing that my greatest nightmare was just ahead of me. I was very early that evening; it was my first day on the job, and I did not want to be late. I noticed when I sat down amongst the other waiters, there were five to six Caribbean boys, and the rest were a mix of nationalities, a total of about seventy-five personnel. Every man's eyes were on me. That was the way they looked on a new guy. Then the question was being asked: Who is the new boy? They all wanted to know where I was from, but only a few would come over and introduce themselves. One of them happened to be my countryman. He sat with me and asked a lot of questions about back home. As I turned around to look on all the new faces, it was no problem for me to recognize the gays. That certain little group always sat together and would give me that cute smile and look. Soon the dining room manager entered the restaurant. I approached him to introduce myself. I thought I would be shaking the hand of a gentleman, but I later learned that he was a racist. After he asked me my name, he then looked at his crew list and shook his head no. "I don't see your name here for dining room waiter."

"There must be a mistake here," I said. "That's the position I applied for."

He talked to the kitchen steward then checked his list and told me I was a utility man, and I would be working with him. Right away I knew something was very wrong although the kitchen steward seemed to be very nice. We had a small talk about the system. I was very understanding, so I decided to work until the end of the cruise, at which point I would definitely take up the matter with the personnel manager on shore side. The kitchen steward was from one of the islands. In the early days when I started working, you would never find a nationality other than Caribbean or Latin American as a kitchen steward. As my first day continued, I followed the kitchen steward to a locker room. When he opened the locker door, I was surprised to see what my uniform looked like. There were some thick pants and shirts and a pair of water boots just waiting for me; that was my first embarrassment on the job.

After I got dressed, I felt a bit strange. We the Caribbean men should have been treated much better and with respect. We lived here, and the cruise lines sailed in our waters. Why should the Caribbean men work in the kitchen as utility workers while other nationalities worked in the dining room where the income was more profitable? I would appreciate it if all Caribbean heads of government would come together and stop this madness so Caribbean men could make better earnings. My utility pay slip was under four hundred per month. Payday was on the fifteenth and thirtieth of each month. My pay slip showed me under two hundred dollars while waiters of other nationalities, according to their contracts, showed seven hundred per month, as dining room waiter tips could be from five hundred to nine hundred per cruise, depending on the size of one station and how generous the passengers tipped.

On my first day, I entered the kitchen, which would be my working area. I could feel the heat that I would have to endure. I could hear the sound of boiling water and the bubbling of the boiling soup, see the scorching vapor of steam as it entered the ceiling, and smell the food under the chopping knives on the chopping board. There were men running here and there. The working chef was shouting as pots and pans were knocking. Everyone was busy. All kinds of nationalities were working together just to meet their deadline at six o'clock without any confusion. Trying not to get into anyone's way, I carefully moved and worked between them. Because I was very adequate, my job became very easy that night during the long hours of heat and sweat. Thirst became the only discomfort to us as our need for ice water and a very cold beer distracted our minds from a night of consistency. Souring feet and exhausted bodies become a daily routine. One thing that I definitely admired most was the length and width of the kitchen after the rush hour of the main sitting was over and all the cooks take their breaks; ice water and cold beer became top priority. In the meantime, my job was to clean the grill and range, and reset the dinner plates for the second sitting. After this, I joined the rest of the cooks, but I preferred to drink water instead of beer; it's much worse to drink alcohol and feel seasick at the same time. Most of the cooks that I met were from the Caribbean; very few were mixed nationalities. The head chef was from Europe, and the working chef and the rest of the cooks did all the work. It was an excellent experience for anyone who did not have any knowledge of the kitchen arrangement to visit. There could be more than eight different cook stations.

Our break was up, and it was time to face the heat again with the shouting voices of all the waiters as they rushed in to pick up their appetizers. This was my first night on board, and regardless of the embarrassing treatment I received, everything seemed educational. During the rush period, dinner plates were running out. My duty was to restock them very fast, or else the cooks would shout for plates. That was what I was trying to avoid; as I continued to work my way around the cooks. There was this one cook who was a gay man and always bracing himself backwards on me. As I kept on disregarding him, I continued to do my job. Every now and then, I would look at the clock, hoping that the minutes would go faster so I could escape the heat of the night. By nine thirty, the line began to break down because the rush was over. Still, you would find a couple of waiters running back for extra meals. Two to three cooks would stay on the line to serve them. After finishing breaking down and clearing out, I was finished for the night. A different shift came up to take over, the night cleaners. They would get the kitchen clean and ready for breakfast in the morning.

Now that I was free, I wasn't ready for bed just yet. I took a walk inside the dining room to look for some of the Caribbean waiters that I met earlier on in the dining room manager meeting. All the passengers had left the restaurant while the waiters and busboys cleaned up and reset the tables for the midnight buffet. As the room became presentable, they all sat down to enjoy their dinner. There was a table of six with one empty chair. Four of the men were from the Caribbean, and one was from Jerusalem. I sat down facing the Arabian. I started to ask the Caribbean boys a lot of questions about the ship. They were very informative and straightforward in telling me the company's system. I was told and later proved to myself that this company as well as others employed mostly Caribbean and Latin American men for the utility jobs. While the six of us were talking, everyone's hands rested on top of the table. I was keeping a close watch on the Arabian in front of me because he looked gayish. As the conversation got deeper, I realized his hands were getting closer and closer. Suddenly, he reached over to touch my hands. I quickly pulled back my hands to avoid him. I did not make a scene or cause any more embarrassment to myself. I said goodnight and left. I walked to the back of the ship where the fresh air gave me a wonderful feeling. What would have made the night much more beautiful was if the moon was out.

That night, most of the crew came to the back of the ship to relax where we could get away from the air conditioning, the heat, the problem, and the confinement. At the back of the ship, I observed everything that was going on. I noticed that which was hidden. Not only did the crew come to the back at night to relax but also to get involved in their nightly activities such as playing music, smoking pot, sniffing hard drugs, and drinking rum and beer. Others came to read the paper or to meet single passenger ladies. There were those who had a girlfriend working on board. They would meet each other at the back, and the guys who didn't have a girlfriend were trying to find one. The gays tried to create the most excitement at the back. What I did notice is that not everybody associated with each other. Each group of nationalities sat or stood by themselves talking. Some definitely did not like to mix with others. Some crew members listened to their walkman radios with the expectation not to be disturbed. Others were playing tape recorders on the other side of the back. I could hear all different kinds of music that night from all over the world. Not all the crew members could stay up and party all night. I noticed they started to leave one by one; those who could stay up longer would surrender by 2 AM. The first patrol made their regular circle and watched to see if anyone was making problems. A crew off-duty tended to get drunk at times.

As the night was getting later, I decided to take a walk down to the crew bar, maybe four or five decks down. The only thing about the crew bar I didn't like was the heavy smoking inside. Rum, beer, and soft drinks were very cheap. Sometimes we would play bingo to enjoy ourselves. If a television was in your cabin, it was best to stay there and watch a movie; if not, you could sit in the showroom. It was not convenient to everyone because most of the crew would fight over the television by turning from one channel to another. It was to our advantage as a crew and much more private to have our own appliances and an ice box in which to keep our beers. I was new at the time, so I definitely kept my distance.

After I retired that night, I decided to go to my cabin to change and take a shower before going to bed. Showering without slippers was not recommended because of athlete's foot.

I learned a lot on my first day. I almost believed there was one nationality employed by the company; everyone was using the same dialect. I was confused after observing all the crew members and how different they looked, yet they used one language. Only in American would you find so many different nationalities working together, but curiosity caused me to ask one important question. "What accent is this you speak?" I asked.

"Jamaican," everyone would answer. Some would say, "It's yardy, man." I was still confused because there was this little blend that mixed up their tongues to make me believe they were lying to me. Before that night was over, unexpectedly I ran into some speaking their own national language. What could they do but laugh, knowing that they were taking me for an ass? I knew and associated with Jamaicans for so long, I later realized why people loved the Jamaican accent. It carried a sweet melody within and was easy to adopt. This was one accent frequently used by criminals as a camouflage to protect their true identity with the intentions to give Jamaicans a bad reputation, both to Jamaicans and their country. Many times I heard crew members speaking to passengers in a Jamaican accent. Even though it was not their accent, they still tried to be nice because it was done in person. By phone, these crew members were not so nice. Every country that I visited, people loved to use the Jamaican indecent language. These words were frequently used by the crew. It was so educational for me to learn the different kinds of indecent words; it really benefited me in a unique way since I worked amongst more than twenty-five different nationalities. Actually, every day there was an argument between the men that led to a fight, which was often triggered by an indecent word, though not all the time. The chef and the maitre d' sometime couldn't get along because of some small detail. Whenever things got out of proportion, then the adopted cultural indecent language caused a scene.

Chapter-4

Anyway, the next morning would be the second day on the ship. My first day at sea, I awoke at 6 AM and started out for work. Usually not a big breakfast person, I only drank a glass of orange juice and ate one slice of french toast. The kitchen was very peaceful and calm. There was not much action in the morning because most passengers hung out too late in the disco, the casino, or the midnight buffet. The ones we considered greedy would come down to the restaurant for breakfast. The ship could look like an empty ghost town when everyone was asleep. There was nothing much to do at 8:15 AM, so the cooks would take a walk to the back, just sit down, and take some fresh air or smoke. It was my first day at sea, and I could see land far off on the starboard side. I stood next to a cook and asked him, "What island is that?"

He told me, "That's Cuba."

I said, "Really?"

He said to me, "You don't know Cuba?"

I answered, "I only read about the place." It was a pleasure to see the dolphins in the early morning when they took their regular flip, the first time that morning. I saw some flying fish from a distance. I thought they were birds. When our twenty-minute break was up, we cleared the deck and headed straight for the kitchen, one behind the other. We opened the line and waited for the waiters; the arrangement of service tool, and the cooks took their original places. The head breakfast cook stayed in the back where he made omelets and special orders.

As the door that separated the dining room from the galley opened, suddenly the shouting began. All the waiters came rushing out to pick up their appetizers. There was always confusion amongst them because most of them could hardly read and write in English properly. Their behavior was far below standard. Their custom was to push one another in the line and fight. As one waiter turned around, the other from behind would steal his plate—cover or tray. Indecent language between them was a common practice. For such a reason, most of the time, the cooks and waiters would get into big arguments. Even if the waiter was wrong, the first thing he would do was run and make a complaint to the dining room manager with a false story. He would return and expect to be right. Where there was no self-respect, there was no regard for another. The low morale and mentality these mixed-nationality boys produced made me wonder why existence every walk thier way. Profanity and mental deficiency - things I saw and heard every day. I was not a racist, but spiritually I withdrew from them so I could keep my morals that the true God above had instilled in me.

As soon as breakfast was over and the passengers had finished eating, the busboys would come out to wash all the dirty dishes and utensils for the re-setting of the dining room. In the galley, their behavior was the same as the waiters'. Every busboy wanted his plate to be washed first, then the pushing would start. Problems always arose between them because one would forget the number of his silver rock. The rock would come out at the other end of the washing machine, and he would take any one he believed was his. The rightful owner would step forward and demand his rock according to his number. Then a war would develop between the two busboys; this fight would not stop until three or four busboys got between them. The next thing you knew, the utensils were on the floor and had to go through the wash again. One thing I learned about these disputes was that if a Caribbean boy was involved, he would get the blame over the other nationalities even if he was right.

Now that the galley staff had started their cleaning up too, they would make their own breakfast plus for some of the waiters and cabin stewards who loved island food. The cook didn't charge anyone for a single plate, but normally some of the guys would show their appreciation at the end of the cruise. I believed he deserved it because their monthly salaries, including mine, were far too low below standard. Most of the breakfast cooks who started out very early in the morning did not have to work for dinner, so to make extra money to take care of their families, they became cabin steward helpers. As helpers, their job was to clean the bathroom toilet bowl, change the towels, replace fruit and ice, and vacuum the carpet for ten dollars per night. Some guys would do drugs. I didn't blame them because they didn't have a choice. I did feel sorry for them when they got caught though. Were we still in a stage of mental slavery?

There were crew members who got hold of master keys. Some would make duplicates at shore side then break into your cabin while you were at work. The second night after we finished working, I went to my cabin and found it empty. I looked out my door, and there was not a soul to be found. "Maybe," I said, "the crew is in the crew bar partying." I took a shower and got dressed. On my way to the crew bar, I entered through the door with the expectation of finding everyone. I was surprised to find only the bartender alone. "Where is everybody?" I asked.

"Up on deck," he said.

"Doing what?" I asked.

He replied, "We arrive in Port Antonio tomorrow morning."

I said, "Okay. I'll see you later." I then made my way up the deck to the back of the ship. When I got there, I could not believe my own eyes. All different kinds of nationalities were there. I simply moved around to mingle because I was still a new boy. I never knew that Jamaicans could be so happy when sailing down to their country. That night they bought all the beers and had a big party. The music box was a big tape recorder attached to a long extension cord. During certain hours in the morning, they would try to pick up the radio station and tune into the reggae music. Most of the crew stayed up all night drinking and dancing. Most Jamaicans didn't work the next morning; they were off for the rest of the day until dinner. There were those who would go home to see their families or girlfriends, and there were those who wouldn't have any of the above. These were the playboys; a girl in every port was their desire. In Jamaica, the ship became a ghost town; everybody was on shore. Jamaica was a very attractive place to visit. Passengers and other crew members from Europe alike would go to the beach all day to lie in the sun, while some would take a tour and afterward do some shopping. The Caribbean crew was totally different. These guys would find the action spot like the bar and the day club. They wanted girls and more girls, but these girls were working-class girls; they could not be run over easily. At the time, I didn't believe in settling down. Yet I had the worst taste for prostitutes, but generally speaking, it was the seaman's practice to have a woman in each port. I met a lot of girls in my first year as a seaman. I learned for myself that some of these island girls loved foreigners while some didn't. Seamen liked to shop a lot so it was their desire to impress the sales lady by purchasing one of the most expensive items. Every cruise he would purchase from the same store so that the relationship would get stronger. If he saw that there was an opportunity there for him, he would ask her out for lunch.

As our stay in Jamaica for the day was winding up, I proceeded to one of the best day clubs with some of my close friends. As I sat to have a cold Red Stripe, I watched every move they made with the prostitutes. Out of nowhere, one prostitute came over and slid right between my legs and asked me, "Do you want to take me to the hotel for the day?"

I told her, "Depends on how much."

She said, "Twenty U.S. dollars."

I always cried them down each time one approached. It was like a joke to me because going to bed with a prostitute was against my principles. Back then was the good old days when you could get the best-looking prostitute for twenty U.S. dollars, but now you cannot afford them anymore. However, that day I tried not to become too popular.

I studied the behavior of the crew. There was one who loved to spend very heavily; he was the type who loved attention. There was another who loved to talk plenty. The next one loved to boast. There was another one who loved to dress fussy like only he knew how to wear good clothing. The next guy wanted you to believe he had more money than anybody else. There were a few guys that the police loved to check because they were always full of gold chains and rings. There was a guy who went ashore just to rent a car and came back to show off to everybody that he could drive. He was parked this minute, and the next minute he would jump in, back out of the parkway, burn some tire, speed up, and drive down the road trying to kill somebody. A lot of madness took place for one day. As the day moved on, half the crew were already drunk, and a lot of money had been spent.

By 4 PM that evening, every crew member headed back for the ship, the drunk and the sober. You should have seen these men marching back with a left and a right. The town became peaceful and calm because all crew members had to be back on board half an hour before sailing time. If the ship sailed without you, company policy was an immediate dismissal. If the reason was serious, then you had a good chance to be excused. I never once intended to go too far. I liked an easy walk back to the ship. I have experienced many times that the ship left a crew member behind, and that was not a good feeling. Some crew members took it for a sport. If he was a good liar and could come up with a good excuse, the job was his. Some crew members were not so lucky. A crew member left behind had to contact the ship agent at once. There was a number provided for us on the back of our identification crew pass. It was the agent's duty to book you into a hotel until the ship returned the following cruise. Sometimes the main office would order the agent to fly the crew member to the next port of call to join the ship. Immediately after the crew member arrived, he had to see the captain at once, but he had to be a good liar in defending himself. If the job was his, he would only pay a fine and receive a final warning. Once everybody was back on board at 4 PM from a long sporty day, all the crew members went to the back to watch the ship set sail, and while we were there, everybody started to talk about the day's events. I would stand there and listen to them talking their mouths off about where they went, what they did, and on and on. All these guys talked about was women and what they did to them and how many girls they had sex with and what style and position they played in bed.

Chapter-5

As we set sail for the next port of call, Grand Cayman, Jamaica became smaller with distance between us and the sea. The deck started to get clearer as everyone had to start working. As the sun looked like it was going down into the ocean, the evening started to look restful, and the cool breeze started to blow from the north to the south while we were going west. I almost fell asleep that evening. "Tomorrow is a long day for us," I said to myself. "So, after dinner tonight, I must study my safety booklet because the officers will be asking me questions about safety at the boat drill."

As soon as a new crew member signed on, he was informed by the head of the department to pay a visit on the bridge the next morning where the safety officer was waiting to meet him. A safety booklet and a life jacket would be issued to each crew member as his personal property until he signed off the vessel. A speech would be given by some safety officer, while others liked to give a tour—it depended on the cruise line. The safety booklet was to be studied and to be taken seriously. Each individual's life depended on what we knew in case of an emergency. Some crew members took it for a joke though there were disciplinary measures for such action. I personally preferred the touring of the ship over the speech. A tour around the ship was very educational. The safety officer during the tour took the new sign-on floor by floor and pointed out every piece of safety equipment then explained it in full detail, regardless of the regular drill we had once per week and a constant check of the United States Coast Guard every three months. Still, some crew members only cared about themselves. Every drill, there was a crew member absent. Some were on the excuse list, while some weren't, but where safety was concerned, there would always be a couple of crew members who would ask the head of the department to put them on the excuse list so that they could go ashore on their personal business. If each department head did the same, we might have ended up short twenty men, plus the men who were entitled to the excuse. Some stations did not check by offices or anyone; when a fire emergency occurred, whistles were blown. Most crew members knew that their emergency stations never checked. They would lay in bed instead of picking up their life jackets and proceeding to their positions where their duty was to check all the cabins to see if any passengers were left inside and if so, to direct them up to the embarkation deck. While some crew members goofed off in their cabins, the safety officer conducted a cabin-to-cabin check because he knew that there were crew members hiding from the drill. When the crew members were caught, they would have to face the full penalty of a fine. After the third time, such crew members would receive the full measure of dismissal. The crew that conducted the checking at the boat station had many friends. Whenever a friend was absent from such a drill, he would mark him present for the drill.

Not every crew member read his booklet. Even if he did, not every crew member had a photographic memory, and it was fun for me to watch them struggle when they were asked a question by the officer. We expected the Coast Guard at the end of the cruise. We began training on how to lower the life raft so that the Coast Guard would believed that we were a top-shape team, but after the Coast Guard drill was over, most of the crew forgot everything. That was why it was essential to conduct a boat drill every week. Sometimes I laughed when crew members moved from one side of the ship to another searching for their boat station. It was important to all of us as a crew and of great interest to the passengers when the crew was well prepared.

Most officers failed to show the crew respect. Officers always thought they were gods. All they did at the drill was shout at us and bark like a dog spun around like a fool. At the same time, they wanted you to be afraid of them. The lowest thing an officer could do depended on which one of the cruise lines it was.

At the general drill was a female crew member who was new. This officer, this nincompoop, would target this poor girl and ask her straining questions. He knew she could not answer him. He knew she was new, and when anyone is new, it takes a good month to memorize this booklet. Some crew members may do it in less than a month; it all depends on how hard you worked and how tired you felt. Some crew members' photographic memories were sharper than others', and if I was an officer, I would be the one who would have the proper insight and go easy on this newcomer. Instead of being rough, he should have insisted that the individual study her safety booklet more often. That day at the drill, the officer told the girl to see him in his office. He normally told everyone that, but we the crew that day knew that he was up to something. We the crew knew that when this girl reached his office, the subject would change from safety to a more personal conversation. I disrespected officers who portrayed this kind of attitude. I have learned that not only the crew showed carelessness but the officers too.

The ship was a very safe vessel to be on only if all the crew members took safety seriously. The only time I found the crew not wandering around but standing in a straight line was when the Coast Guard was on board.

I noticed that every officer would ask us the same question, and when we answered, the officer would ask us, "What is the abandon ship signal?"

I would answer him, "One short blast from the ship horn or whistle."

He asked me, "How long have you been here and you still don't know the answer?" He told me that it was seven short blasts followed by one long blast. "I don't care what is written in the safety booklet." They kept on asking confusing questions.

At the drill, the shorter men liked to stay in the back line to avoid being asked questions by the officer, but normally I stepped aside so the officer could see them. If the safety officer disliked you, he was going to pick on you at every drill.

In case of a real emergency, some of us were trained to inflate the life craft and lower the lifeboats to the water. We also learned to operate the crane. Still, our real danger was fire. There were several fire warning devices all over the ship, and it was important to remember the special number to call the bridge when there was an emergency duty and fire zone. We also trained to use fire hoses and extinguishers. We also learned about the three kinds of fire: A, B, and C classes. We also trained to use A, B, and C brand extinguishers, CO_2 brand extinguishers, or water— depending on the type of fire. We were trained to operate the watertight door and study all the equipment in the lifeboat. A special training drill took us one hour of studying life-saving equipment. I personally found it to be educational. One fact that I observed amongst the crew was that life was very important to everyone. Consciously speaking, if there was a real and sudden tragedy where panic and confusion became the shadow of death, every man would be in a scrambled position instead of a based position.

As we arrived in Grand Cayman the next morning, the island looked very small and quiet and carried a lot of banks. The town was very small and of no great interest to the crew. As a crew, we didn't have much to see or do in Grand Cayman. The first thing any seaman wanted to do when he was in port was to find a nice place to relax and to sit down and have a drink and for once forget about the ship's hard work and the problem givers. It was also nice to get away from the air conditioning and grip your first breath of fresh air. With all the expectations that we had for Grand Cayman, we could not find any place to fulfill our needs. Passengers could go just about any where to enjoy themselves because their vacation was in progress. They did not carry any burden on their shoulders like we the crew did. As soon as we got on shore, the first thing a crew member did was look at his watch then decide how many hours he would like to spend. Whenever we were off, we looked for a day club or disco to entertain ourselves. Time would always be short and against us, and what we were looking for here we didn't find. For this reason, Grand Cayman was not our favorite port as seamen. We did less shopping there because we the crew found it to be very expensive.

Somewhere around 5 PM that evening, we set sail for Mexico, for a small island off the mainland called Cozumel; it was a very nice island. The first thing I noticed that morning as we arrived was the flies that stormed the outdoor restaurant we called the snack pantry. Because the food was already exposed, we could not spray them. The only thing that we did was fan them off the food, and the more we fanned, the closer they got. Although these germ-carriers pitched on top of the sweet rolls and scrambled eggs and other items, the passengers sat down and ate like nothing was happening without any concern. I had to wonder that morning if flies were a part of their diet. Puerto Rico and Saint Thomas also carried a lot of flies.

That same afternoon while I was walking with a certain crew member, I witnessed something very troubling and misleading, and it really broke my heart. The crew member that I was walking with was a shoplifter. One thing I learned very fast was that you don't play around in any Spanish-speaking country. The police, they don't joke when you break the law. Right away, I scolded him and went my separate way. From that day on, I preferred to go ashore by myself. After I separated from that thief, I remembered the name of a place that the crew was talking about, so I took a taxi and told the driver where I would like to go. I noticed that the driver had a big smile on his face. I asked him, "What's up?"

He answered, "You jiggy jiggy today."

I asked him, "What's jiggy jiggy?"

He replied, "In English, sex."

I laughed and he laughed too. When we reached the destination, I realized a lot of the ship's crew members were there. "Want me to wait for you?" the driver asked.

"No, thank you," I replied as I entered the building. There were girls everywhere. Some of them had long hair and were very pretty. "I have to sample one of these Mexican girls," I said to myself. I sat with some of the older men from the ship, but I did not tell them about the guy that was shoplifting because I did not want to create an enemy. As I was sitting there, I called over one of the Mexican girls to sit and have a couple of beers together.

She came over and said, "Buenos diaz, amigos."

I simple said hi. She couldn't have been more than twenty because she looked very young. While visiting the new country, I almost forgot my problems on board the ship. I had to remember to check the main office when I returned to the States. As the senorita sat down, I pulled my chair closer to her until they were together so I could put my arms around her and touch her breasts. They felt firm, nice, and small. Her nose was straight as an arrow. Her hair was long, past her shoulders. When I held her around her little fine waist, I felt like I was on top of the world. I had no choice but to question her. "Are you for sale?" I asked.

"No," she answered. I didn't believe her because I was told they all said the same thing when your face showed up for the first time.

The temptation at that very moment was strong, so strong that I could not take it any longer. I suddenly pulled her to the dance floor to break the heat. As I continued dancing, I felt someone tapping me on the right shoulder. He said, "Let's go. It's time to head back to the ship." Instantly I knew I was saved by time because I could not resist this girl. The taxi could only hold five men each.

As I approached the dock, I saw a large crowd standing. I could tell that something was really wrong. You didn't find crew members in big numbers on the dock talking together like this. The first thing to come to my mind was a drug bust, which it was, unfortunately for them. I was sorry that they got caught. Maybe only I alone knew the real reason why I said that. These guys were from one of the Caribbean islands. If they were mistreated at first, that was beyond my knowledge, but for certain, the following cruise, when we returned to Mexico, a group of us went to the police station to investigate. We were told the guys were already in the big house. We then left the station to find the big house, which we did. From the look of this place, we knew right away that these guys were inextricable. We spoke to them for a while until one burst out in tears; he could not help it. When we asked what the problem was, then out came the truth: They were mistreated. I asked, "In what way?"

One of them answered that at night, the prison guard would go out, get drunk, then come back just to have sex with them. Tears filled my eyes immediately when I heard these words. I always felt sorry for someone when something dreadful happened to them. But this was the very first time I felt what real sorry was. We spent a long time talking with them, but it was time to leave because there were other things to do. This special day brought one thing to my mind, and I always cherished it: Say no to drugs. Other men passed through that day with drugs without being spotted by the police, but I considered them very lucky because whenever there was a drug bust, the security on the dock became stricter and ready for any crack down. But the drug traffickers would change their techniques in transporting the drugs.

I had in mind to go back and visit the same girl that I met the cruise before, but the day started out bad for me after visiting the big house. As the time kept ticking away, I decided to go back on board. While I was on board, I played a little detective. I spotted the ring lord talking with others. It was like the knights at the round table. As I sat down far off, I looked at them. They had to be reorganizing themselves from the look of things. I did not want to get too close to any of these guys or have them suspect me of watching them. I had learned a lot in less than three minutes. It was very educational to watch these men and study all their drug moves, but this free lesson would have to be delayed until some other time because I had my own problem to take care of in two days when I arrived in the States.

Chapter-6

As we sailed out of Mexico, our destination lay ahead. With one day and two nights at sea, the only company that traveled with us was the ocean that rocked us from left to right and the depth that stayed beneath tons of steel. If my memory serves me correctly, every last day we had a captain inspection on board. This inspection included all departments. This was the day we all worked the hardest, and the hours were a little longer than normal. A captain's duty was not only to sail the ship but to keep the ship clean and to make sure everything was in perfect order. If any section of the ship, internal or external, needed to be repaired, this was observed by his inspection instantly. A.V.O. would be written up and sent to the maintenance team to check out and repair the next day, and the job was normally done. While inspecting the hotel department, the captain would walk the floors. He would check the cabins section by section. Each cabin steward carried fourteen to twenty cabins in his section, and in each section, at least three cabins should be ready for the captain to conduct his inspection. The bathroom and walls would be checked to make sure they were properly scrubbed and clean. The curtain would be checked for mildew, and the captain would pass his hands all over the cabin searching for dust. He checked beneath the bed to see if it had been vacuumed properly. He also checked the portholes and air conditioning. Then he moved to the next section. The bar would be checked also, and all the equipment used to make drinks would be tested to see if they were sanitized. The captain knew exactly what he was looking for. Of all the departments that were checked on this day, the dining room would receive the most thorough check. The last area to be checked was the crews' quarters, and we had over twenty-five different nationalities living together. The messiest cabins on inspection day were those of the mixed nationalities. Their beds were always unmade, and the bed linens needed to be changed. The rules stated that bed linens had to be changed once per week. If the cabin was accompanied by smokers, their ashtray was never cleaned, and cigarette butts could be found beneath the beds. The mirror was so filthy that you could hardly see yourself. When shaving in the basin, these guys never cleaned up behind themselves. Their clothing should have been properly arranged; instead, clothing could be found all over the cabin. Their cabin always failed the captain's inspection.

Crew members that were from Asia loved to eat plenty of rice, so they would provide for themselves a crock pot to cook rice in, which used electricity. These oriental-looking people were from every country in Asia. While walking through the corridor, you could smell cooked rice. The clever ones would first use some masking tape and neatly tape around the door to prevent fellow crew members or officers from detecting them. Those from India would bring food down to the living quarters too like rice and curry. Because curry was very staining, their cabin always smelled like a curry mill. The European waiter who had a girlfriend on board always took food to her cabin, and this was what caused the roaches to multiply. The roaches lived behind the cabin walls, and they all came out at night to feed. When the roaches were overpopulated, both day and night, they could be found crawling all over the cabin. They could be seen in your bed, your clothing, down the hallway, and everywhere. Roaches could dominate the whole ship for this reason. On inspection day, the captain would not find any evidence of cooking, regardless of these crew members-

-Cabins were a prime suspect the day before crew quarters' inspection. A general cleaning took place by the cabin mates to ensure no evidence was left behind. The crew was always smarter than the captain. At all times, it was of great interest to the company that the captain inspected and re-inspected the vessel to make sure the whole ship was completely clean. Some ships', especially the older ones', crew areas were in very bad condition. As soon as the captain was finished, everything went back to normal until the last night of the cruise, when all departments had to re-clean, which was wash, rinse, and sanitize and stay ready in case a United States public health officer paid us a visit.

Chapter-7

Now that everything was over and done with, and everyone seemed relaxed, the anxiety was still in me. I could hardly wait to see the next day. I wanted to know what chance I had face to face with the main office who called themselves big shots though they were just lumps of clay. The night before arrival, I did not get much sleep. I was thinking too much about whether my position would be changed. Fortunately, I awoke the next morning to a morning that many people did not get the opportunity to see. I was happy to see a new day. After finishing my work that morning, I took a shower and then got dressed to look presentable.

After I approached the main office, I pushed the door. "Good morning," I said to everybody. Not everyone answered, in a way that I could understand. I asked for the personnel manager, and I was directed to him. "Good morning," again I said.

He said, "Good morning, sir. What can I do for you, sir?"

"I came to talk to you about my contract, sir," I answered.

"Sit down, he said. He then pulled his file and picked out some information about me. Then he opened it and started to read it by himself. After doing so, he lifted up his eyes and looked at me and said, "You know, you are right, sir. Your contract says here snack steward."

I said to myself, "What in the hell is snack steward?" I said bravely to him, "What is that?"

He answered, "A cafeteria where you will serve breakfast and lunch."

I said, "But, sir, I applied for a waiter position in the dining room."

The living dead replied to me, "We don't have any position for a waiter right now. I will see what I can do for you later on."

He called a lady who looked like a real redneck. You didn't have to ask any questions; you could see it printed out right on her face. She asked me to follow her to her office. She then called the head chef, and he entered the office too. In my presence, the chef was told to see to it that I was moved from kitchen duty. She told the chef I should not be working with him. I shook her hand and said, "Thank you very much."

She replied, "You are welcome."

I left the office and went back over to the dock where most of the men hung out instead of going into town. On the dock, all different kinds of people came there to make a day of living the good, the bad, and the evil. The good were those who came to earn an honest living so that they could take care of their family, if they had one. There used to be a lady every week who would sell movies to the crew, and in those days, most ships did not carry a satellite dish. Therefore, most crew members loved to buy movies from her. She would also sell us great reggae music. There were a few meals on wheels as well. As soon as we got off the ship, these food trucks would be waiting for us, and this was where most of us had our breakfast. There were other people who sold different things like clothing, jewelry, and appliances. There was this Cuban businessman there at all times. I noticed his daughter worked with him. Her legs were not so great, but I still told her she had the best pair of legs I had ever seen. She was really impressed. Her father realized that I was talking with her too much, and for that reason, he never came back to the dock to sell again. The other good guys who stayed around us were the plainclothes police who said that they were undercover watching out for any wrong move. If they were undercover, no one should have been able to spot them that easily, but we always spotted them. It only took one man to recognize them, and the word would go around very fast on the dock. We had to watch out for taxi men in any big city because they were pros … they had the proper instinct to detect a newcomer when they arrived at the airport. They never asked you for your destination at first; they waited until you got in and moved off. To distract you, the driver would ask you all different kinds of questions before he asked you where you would like to go. It was best to tell the address from your memory. If you looked for a piece of paper that contained your address, he knew for sure that he got you at the end of the rope. Unfortunately, because you were a newcomer, this driver was going to take the longest route so he could run up the meter, and you ended up paying more than the usual cost. On top of everything, they normally asked for tips.

After a number of years passed by, I started to get used to the city and how much it cost from point A to point B. Learning the city very fast made a big difference. I could tell the driver which road I preferred to travel on. Because we were crew members, the taxi drivers loved to drive on the road that carried the most stop lights.

Also there were those who came down to the dock every day a crew ship was in to sell stolen jewelry and wash over gold. Anyone who came to the States for the first time was innocent to the environment around them. There was a price every newcomer had to pay in order to know the ropes. You were natural prey, ready to be exploited. I got caught once, and that was enough. This guy came up to me so smoothly. In his hand, I saw a handkerchief. He opened it and showed it to me for about five seconds. It was a gold ring. Then he quickly pushed it back into his pocket. I was reluctant to purchase the ring, so he showed it to me once more. The ring looked good. I told him yes.

He answered, "This is the best deal you can get. This is fourteen-karat gold plus six diamonds on top for only twenty dollars." As soon as he received my twenty dollars, he took off with speed. Still I did not suspect anything. I figured more than the less he was otherwise hot. One month later, I noticed that the ring started to change color. That was the moment I started to realize the significance of his speed. I have learned my lesson not to buy jewelry from guys on the street.

My cabin mate went through the same experience after buying a television from one guy on the dock. His appearance told us that he was a drug addict and only needed some fast cash to supply his needs. After my cabin mate purchased the television, he then opened the box. "A nice-looking television," he said. "I need to test it on board to see if it is working. It feels kind of heavy for a normal television." As soon as we reached the cabin, my cabin mate plugged it in. I heard him say something was wrong.

"What do you mean something is wrong?" I said. "This is a new television." So we both rushed outside to tell the guy that the television was broken, but he was long gone. We then asked the ship technician to check out our new appliance because there was a fault. The technician removed the back of the television, and to our surprise, the television was full of bricks. Everybody started to laugh. My cabin mate got upset and rushed out again to find the guy. I considered the guys on the dock to be evil. Their presence alone could be interpreted as death, judgment, and unpleasantness. I could smell riches, followed by power and a dead hero. In due time, these kinds of guys drove expensive cars. As soon as more than one of these guys entered the dock, I moved from the area; in case of a shootout, I could take proper cover. Oftentimes, I sat down and observed the pickup man come, and the delivery man could not be found on such occasions. I tried to mind my own business and not give any reason for someone to kill me. Neither would I want to move from the spot; they might have thought that I was a part of the conspiracy. This was the first time that I started to study drug movements in the early eighties until the retirement of my career.

Sitting on the dock, no crew members needed to read their watches to know when it was time to go back on board. We noticed that the taxis were leaving rapidly. The visitors were driving off. One by one, the food trucks were packing up to go, and the bad boys were nowhere to be found. The drug pushers moved off with speed, leaving their tire marks behind them, and all of a sudden, the whole area became quiet.

I left the others and went back on board because I normally loved to take a nap before work. An hour and a half was enough for being on my feet for actually the whole day. I remembered to get up at 5 PM. I was running late, but still decided to take a shower. Wearing slippers was a must. I happened to pick the wrong shower that evening. I stepped in something and almost fall backwards. After I regained my balance, I bent down to investigate what the obstacle was. I found out that someone or the last person to use the shower had just finished masturbating and forgot to wash out the bathroom floor. I was not the first one to make such a complaint. I suspected all the guys who did not have a girlfriend on board or in port.

After the shower, I got dressed. I went up to the kitchen to ask the chef if my position had changed. This would be my second cruise, and I didn't intend to experience another week inside the kitchen, especially with that gay guy who always pushed up against me when I passed by. Fortunately, I was moved inside the dining room as a buffet runner with the belief that I would still keep quiet. This new position that I now held was under the portfolio of utility, and I realized the discrimination against me. I remained a buffet runner for two years. Being a buffet runner, my responsibilities were essential to the health of the passengers and crew. My new duty and schedule started all over again. I was still willing to try something new, anything to get away from the kitchen. Still, I was not deeply touched, because it was three meals a day when we were at sea and two meals a day when we were in port. I had one day off per week, which was not a full day. I only got the lunch off, and by five fifteen, I started to set the buffet again. Because there were two buffet runners, the lunch off had to be rotated. So the next port would be his day off.

Breakfast in the dining room started at seven thirty in the morning. To be on time, I had to be out of bed no later than six o'clock. My body temperature would drop when taking a cold shower. After I got groomed, I hit the stairway that led to the kitchen, where I picked up all my material to set up the buffet. After turning on the buffet, it took at least twenty minutes for the surface to become frozen. On my far right, I laid out the juices, seven different kinds. Next to the juice was all the citrus, and across to my left, I laid out all the hot and cold cereals. We opened seven thirty sharp for the passengers' dining pleasure, and at eight fifteen, we closed the door again to reset the dining room. We packed the buffet for the second seating at eight forty-five. While I sat down to rest my legs during the break, I watched the Europeans come up to the buffet that was ready and waiting for the passengers. They used their fingers to take food or anything they wanted to eat. It was against public health regulations for so many hands without gloves touching and moving food. There were plenty of opportunities for the items to get contaminated after handling clean and dirty utensils, moving and arranging chairs, handling dirty trays, taking a smoke on the stairway, and touching the railing, which was everybody's pathway, and to come over and touch the food.

As the second seating now began, the waiters approached again to pick up their appetizers. I knew that I was not approved by this system to be a professional dining room waiter, but I still took pleasure in teaching a lot of waiters during their first cruise. Some of them successfully learned the name of the juices and could identify them in tasting because of me. While I was standing by the buffet, I watched the waiters pick up the juice and put it to their faces first. If they could not identify by looking first, they would turn to me and ask me, "What juice is this?" Normally, when a waiter forgot something either off the buffet or inside the kitchen, he would ask me to bring it for him. As soon as breakfast was finished, I would take all the leftovers to the kitchen and put them in their respective areas. I would return and clean up the buffet and reset it for lunch. Generally I did what most men would do after breakfast—go straight to bed for a two-hour rest before lunch. Lunch was always busy at sea and could be hectic at times.

Although my monthly salary was under four hundred dollars at that time, still I did not envy anyone. With all the money that these waiters earned, more than half their earnings went down the drain, and the thing that took away their money mostly was drugs. Because it was not free, they had to pay for it. Plus they could play the private casino in the cabin without the knowledge of management. Plus the casinos on shore side liquidated these guys' earnings. Prostitutes, sporting, and nightlife also took away their money and cost them a lot. And none of the above ever bothered these guys because they knew that at the end of every cruise, they could depend on their tips of about five hundred. Of the pay slip that I received at the end of the month I would use one hundred dollars to buy clothing and other items that had run out, and the balance of my earnings I would save to meet the next payday so I could put them together and send it home. There were times I wanted to go ashore, but I did not see any sense in doing so with a broken pocket. Many times I just stayed up on deck and just looked outside. If the town was near I would definitely take a walk instead of using a taxi.

As a buffet runner, money is not walking my way, so something had to be done soon. It had been too long now working in the same position and not making any money, and with the pressure I was giving management for a waiter position, I was moved from the dining room to a different department called snack pantry. The pay was the same, but I was told that in this position it was much easier to be promoted to the dining room as a busboy.

At the snack pantry, my worst nightmare and struggle began. It was the type of men that I had to work with, the head snack steward and my supervisor, and it was all because I was a new boy in this area. I'd rather be straightforward and say that this was the worst supervisor that I had ever run into and he was a gay oriental man. We just could not get along. Our relationship carried a long distance between us, and because of this, my treatment from him became unfair. I had talked to gays that were very good friends of mine. Because I disagreed with the uncivilized approach of this oriental gay man, I started to feel unwelcome and uncomfortable in my new department. In the mornings for breakfast, I would stand in the line and serve scrambled eggs and bacon to the passengers, which was not a big deal. Unexpectedly, my supervisor removed me and sent me to the back to wash dishes and carry out garbage. On several occasions, this serpent came around the back just to give me a hard time about the plates not being washed properly or told me that the floor had to be kept cleaner than it was and the walls had to be washed down whenever I was finished with the dishes. It was pure pressure, and that was all I ever received. There was a glass door that separated the outside floor from the inside, and all this faggot did was stand behind the glass door and admire my ass. Each time I turned around and caught him, he would turn away his head like he was not looking at me. In various ports, this gay boy who was the assistant food and beverage manager normally liked to go out for lunch.

With some of the other boys. I said to myself, "If this is the only way for me to get popular on board, this faggot has another thing coming." What I noticed was that they didn't care what they did wrong; these gays always had a godfather to protect them, and for this reason, they behaved like they were the owners of the vessel. The older guys with seniority had a better chance of keeping their jobs than a new guy like me. In my department, because I was a new guy, the other men that I worked amongst smartly gave me some of their work. It was beyond my knowledge that in this system, that happened to every new guy that came on board. This kind of wrongdoing would continue until a new boy learned his way out. Not one of these guys would ever show me a little sympathy by helping me out in the back. On the other hand, if the outside became busier than they could handle, the head snack steward would come in the back and ask me to help out impolitely. I did it without a murmur. I always liked to think ahead of them by not giving anyone the chance whatsoever to make any kind of complaint wrongfully against me.

There were two gay men in my department; one was the supervisor, and the other was a snack steward from one of the Caribbean islands. Most of the time when we were in port, the both of us would be on the same duty While in port, there was nothing much to do because all the passengers were on shore, sitting around doing nothing On this particular morning, surprising to me, this little unwanted gay man who should have died at birth was spinning around me. I guessed he was doing this because he felt hot in the morning. Unfortunately for him, the supervisor faggot was not around. Normally on board you could tell when gay boys had just finished mating; they walked funny and carried an awful smell. I was strictly determined not to eat or drink from any one of these guys.

At the end of every cruise in the pool café, which we called snack pantry, the whole team would break down the complete area and conduct a complete wash and sanitization from top to bottom, preparing ourselves in case a surprise public health inspector should come on board. Very early the next morning, while approaching the United States port, the captain, the hotel manager, staff captain, chief engineer, sanitation officer, chief electrician, and other heads of departments had to conduct a general inspection throughout the ship no later than 6 AM. Right before the ship docked, the United State public health inspector could visit unexpectedly or cruise undercover.

Chapter-8

While I was working in the pantry, I happened to run into a cabin steward who told me he was looking for a helper. I asked him what that was. He said it was someone to clean the bathroom, put up new towels, fill up the ice buckets, vacuum the carpet, and carry down the dirty towels to the laundry when I was finished for the night. I asked the cabin steward how much I would be working for per night. He told me ten dollars per night plus on debarkation morning after the passenger had left the cabin, I would be doing the same thing over again. The only difference was that the last morning would pay fifty bucks. "This is going to be a long day," I said to myself, but I needed the money. I had to suffer the consequences in order to make ends meet. I did take the job, but I didn't know where the energy was going to come from. Anyway, I decided to work for him.

The next morning, I found myself awake and well, and I was off to work up in the pantry, the only outdoor restaurant we had on board. I started out at six o'clock because early bird coffee was at six thirty and breakfast was from seven thirty until ten thirty. After breakfast was over, immediately without any break, we reluctantly reset the pantry for lunch, which was the typical American food—hot dogs, hamburgers, mixed salad, cakes, and pie. We had four different containers that we mixed Kool-Aid in, and at all times, we gave passengers two different flavors to choose from. When it was not time to wash dishes in the back, I would come out front for some fresh air, and I would recognize the same set of faces that ate with us every day. It was terrible to see passengers sit down and drink up to fourteen cups of coffee, and I knew this didn't happen at home. It was not affordable every morning. They would eat the same thing—scrambled eggs, bacon, and sausage. For a change, these passengers should try the dining room for

42

breakfast where they had a wider variety to choose from. These people never changed; they came back to eat the same thing all over again, and with the wide variety of cakes that we put out, the chocolate cake was the first to finish. Before we closed lunch at two, the passengers from the main seating in the dining room would show up for lunch at the pool café, and the passengers from the pool café would go down to the dining room.

Lunch was now over, and every man knew his duty. There were six of us. We took a short break and went down to our cabins to have a fast drink of rum and Coke and rest our feet awhile before we went back to work at three thirty to reset for the afternoon tea, during which we served light snacks and ice cream. As the door opened, I couldn't believe my eyes; it was the same passenger standing outside waiting. We all started to laugh. I asked my colleague why he was laughing too. Who gave him the joke? In my whole life, I had never seen people who could eat like this.

That same evening, when everything was over and done with, I remembered the agreement I made with the cabin steward to be his helper. At five thirty, I sat down in the crew mess to have my dinner and relax for half an hour. At six o'clock, the dining room would be open for the main seating passengers. Then the cabins would be empty for cleaning. With all this time I had been around these kinds of people, I was surprised to learn for myself that some passengers were filthy and sloppy. Starting in the bathroom, I got a bucket with soap and water and a scratchpad to rub the bathroom walls. Despite the heavy grease, I managed to get the job done. the way I learned. To dry the bathroom walls I used the same dirty towels that needed to go to the laundry. Next was the toilet. I couldn't understand why they had to leave the toilet unflushed, like the only toilet these people were used to was the pit toilet where they didn't have to pull a chain. Each time I entered the bathroom, the first thing I did was flush the toilet. To wash the face basin, I left the pipe running so that the spit they left could be washed out. Then I would shine the mirror. Underwear would be left just about anywhere, whether it was clean or not. I thought to myself that a little pride would be considerate. Another steward called me the same evening to show me the kind of passenger he had to put up with. Whenever his passenger finished using the toilet, he never cleaned his butt with the tissue that was provided for him but went straight and sat on his bed and created a mess. Some passenger cabin stewards had to change sheets every day. For ten dollars per night, I had to go through a whole lot of nastiness in order to make up my salary. With the long hours I now started to put in, I became very tired. Vitamins were the only source of energy I depended on. The problem we Caribbean boys have with the company system is that we don't look for pleasure, neither do we enjoy unhappiness. Whenever pleasure comes but once in a blue moon, we help ourselves.

Chapter-9

The first single female passenger I met turned out to be a bad date. I frequently heard other guys talking about catching the clap from passengers. I could not believe it. I always respectfully looked upon passengers as nice and decent people who took a cruise just to get away from the cold up north and problems and came down south to worship the sun and have a good time, but I overlooked the possibility of any passengers being armed and dangerous. She was kind of fat, but I did not have a choice; it had been over a week since I left home. I was living with my father when I became a seaman. This girl knew what she was doing. She purposely set me up for the kill. I did not have any sea-life experience yet, especially with a foreign girl. She was in her late thirties, and every morning it became her regular practice to visit me at the pool café just to eat scrambled eggs and bacon and talk. Her eyes alone told me she was hot and ready. Still, I could not understand why she had to shake her head no each time I asked for her cabin number. Beyond my knowledge, she was seeing another guy on board and was purposely saving me for the last night of the cruise. Bingo, I got the green light. She never showed for up breakfast. Now the opportunity had come, and there was a phrase that said opportunity comes but once. I was definitely steaming up for this girl, the real kind of way, especially for teasing me for one whole week. Tonight I would give her my full power. I would run on all four engines. Anxiety was killing me; I could hardly wait to see the hours come to enter her cabin. On the last evening, after we finished working, I tried my best to finish fast and send someone with a message to tell the cabin steward that I was feeling sick and would be unable to help him out tonight and that I would try to make it in the morning bright and early. My biggest problem now was the night watchman because company rule was, if I got caught going to a passenger's cabin for sure I would be getting a one-way ticket home plus a security guard to accompany me to the airport just to make sure that I boarded the plane, or else the immigration department would fine the company five thousand dollars if the plane missed me and my whereabouts were unknown, so I had to play it like a thief to reach this cabin. I timed the watchman; he passed every half an hour. With perfect timing, I made it to the door, and I was in.

The next morning I was awakened from the noise outside the door. Both passengers and crew members were moving luggage up and down, banging on the wall. The first thing I asked her to do was look outside the door. She looked up and down the corridor to see if the watchman was coming. If the way was clear, I would pop out very fast. I even forgot to take her address. Three days after, I started to experience something. I knew what it was. I then approached the ship's doctor with a lie that I got this thing on shore. I could not tell him it was a passenger; that would make problems worse for me. Back in the early eighties, the good old days, we never used to hear anything frightening such as AIDS. What happened between me and her I did not make a big deal out of it. What this woman did for me was educate me in a sense that I had to beware of passengers, regardless of beauty; one could be deceived.

Working at the pool café, I started to enjoy it because of one thing. We the snack stewards became so fortunate with single girls on board, it became a regular practice and a rat race for who would be first to get a girl before the other. On duty I had to walk around the pool to pick up all the dirty plates the passengers left behind, but I didn't mind it; here was where the crew members could admire some of the nicest girls lying down in their bikinis getting a tan. We were not terrorizing anyone; we just worked in between them, looking and picking up dirty plates. Unexpectedly,

I looked up on the next deck at who was standing there looking down in a pair of shades; it was the captain himself. I did not feel bad after knowing that the man himself was looking too.

The bartenders, bar waiters, and musicians were the easiest crew members to get a single girl. I would notice whenever a single girl was sitting at the bar too long talking with the bartender while having her drink. Maybe one of them became passionate to the other. If that was the case, really he had a good thing going. A couple of free drinks and this girl was his for the whole cruise. Some girls were clever; they would drink out the bar department while building up their hopes for sex, and later disappoint them. But if she ran into the real old veteran and tried to play smart as if she only wanted to drink free with nothing else behind it, don't worry because she would be drinking some Spanish fly. The other type of girl that cruised just to have fun was no problem whatsoever. Either being served by the bartender or waiter, she would only buy once. The remainder of the cruise, the drinks were on the house. Companies could not stop this no matter how hard they tried, and even if they had many spotters on board to watch, the bar staff always spotted them first and easily. The bar staff were not the only ones on board that behaved like this. We had law keepers such as the officers. Some of them, local crew members like myself, were not permitted in any public area except for those on duty in areas like the passenger nightclub and lounge. Only the ship gods can do so still these officer do have a time limit like 2 AM in the morning. If any one of these officers stayed behind, the security officer would ask them to leave. In their position, they had an allowance credit card. This card lasted for one month. As soon as some officers withdrew from their duties, their top priority was to reach the place in action such as the nightclub where they got the

47

opportunity to flirt with the girls. When the allowance card reached its limit, they would wait until their card had been renewed. Still that did not stop one from having a drink. It depended on how close the relationship was between any officer and a bartender. The officer and his passenger girlfriend would be drinking all night on the house. Ladies cruising by themselves could easily be convinced by a good liar. Most crew members on board could not afford to miss such an opportunity. In order to achieve their gold, I heard crew members denying their families. A single girl generally did not want to hear anything about you being a family man, especially when they were looking for a man for themselves, but that was the price they had to pay when they ran into a man who had not been laid in months. All officers thought they were pussycat bullies and only they should get all the girls. A few girls got lucky with men who were not officers, got married, and took their men off the ship. Some officers always broke the rule and set no example. When they saw a girl that really captured their evil eyes, and she looked substantial, he dared not approach her because she did not look easy or the type he always got around. He would trail her to find her cabin number, or if she used her credit card, as soon as she left the counter, he would ask the bartender to show him the check and write the cabin number off of it.

Unexpectedly, this girl started to receive expensive wine at her room, and at the dining table in the restaurant, the wine steward would bring the wine and the glass over and present it to her with a card stating who it was from. I never learned about this incident until lunchtime by the pool café one day. While we were on a seven-day cruise, somehow this girl managed to see my nametag and called to me as she passed by. Quickly I turned around. I then realized that she was a beauty to look on. "Hello, can I help you?" I asked.

"In a way," she said.

"What seems to be the problem, nice lady?"

Without another word from her, she handed me a business card and said, "Tell me about him."

I took the card and looked at it. To my surprise, it was the man himself, second in command, in my mind I laughed because I just got the opportunity to sink an officer for the first time because they were the only big shots on board—at least, that was what they thought. They could proceed to a lady's cabin without hiding. We the crew had to hide to do so, or else it was a one-way ticket home. "Yes, I can help you." I said. "I can tell you everything you want to know about him. I will be honest and straight with you because you look to be a nice person. I like you and would not like to see any harm come to you."

"No," she replied. "I would not like that either."

I replied, "You see, this guy, this is his regular practice. Every cruise he keeps changing girls like the socks he wears. You are not the first, and you will not be the last. Do you remember the wine he sent?"

"Yes," she replied.

"That was to soften you up. Secondly, you are going to receive a special invitation to attend the captain's cocktail party or repeaters party. After the good treatment is over, he is going to take you up to the bridge to educate you on the navigation system, but little did you know his cabin is just around the corner from the bridge. The next move is his invitation to his cabin, but please if this should happen to you, don't forget to draw a line right where you stand. You are a big girl, and he cannot force you in his cabin. He can lose his job if you complain to the hotel manager, captain or shore side." I suggested to her to go if she got the invitation just to prove a point.

The following morning in Mexico, she came directly to see me. She called me by name and said, "I want to thank you for guiding me. Well, you have proven your point." That same morning she talked to me about going shopping and asked if I would like to accompany her.

"No. I am sorry." She asked me why, and I said to her, "You listen to me before, surely you can listen again. Unfortunately, this guy did not get his chance with you last night. I don't think if he saw both of us walking together downtown that he is going to appreciate it. I can be penalized and sent home."

The only time you found some officer really behaving himself was when his wife was cruising on board. Their suites were large and could accommodate a small family. The officer's family privilege was different from the crews' because their wives could cruise with them in the same cabin, but our families had to stay in the passenger cabins. Plus we had to get permission from upstairs to visit them. You didn't get such access for your girlfriend or any other date. If your girlfriend was cruising, telling your friends should be limited.

One morning in St. Thomas Virgin Island by 10 AM, almost every passenger was gone. Some went on a shopping spree while others took a tour. The whole place was quiet and peaceful. There was just the breeze from the other side of the mountain blowing across us with very few flies. There were three ladies in their middle forties who came down to have breakfast. Unfortunately, time was against them. I instantly apologized in order to prevent them from getting upset. I imagined how hungry and disappointed these three ladies were. I started to converse with one of the ladies. She was the social kind of person, so I did not have any problem communicating. I took her to the side and asked her, "Do you have any plans for today?"

"No," she answered.

I said, "Well, after I am through cleaning up this place, I am going into town."

"To do what?" she asked.

"To get away from the ship for a while, and there is this lovely restaurant that I eat lunch at all the time. The taxi fare is only two dollars a person, and I will make sure that you get back here in one piece, okay?"

"You promise?" she said.

I asked her to meet me at the gangway outside at eleven o'clock. She then turned toward her other friends and told them about our lunch date and that she would catch up with them later. "That is fine with us," the other ladies replied. I rushed off down to my cabin to change as fast as I could. I rushed back up the stairs like a madman to change my crew pass, and off the gangway I went. I looked left then to the right. The lady was not out yet. A voice in my head told me to go back inside. I was right; she was waiting for me inside the gangway. I did not try to correct her or show her, her mistake. "There you are," I said. "Are you ready?"

"Yes," she answered. We both took a taxi into town. After I finished showing her around, we both went for lunch. Neither of us was a big drinker, so two cocktails each before lunch was enough. We each had a shrimp salad for lunch. On the way back to the ship, I invited her to my cabin for a drink. It was 9 PM. That same evening, after she finished eating dinner, she came to my cabin. It was safer coming to my cabin than going to hers. All I did was ask my cabin mate to help me pilot her in. As soon as she was in, my cabin mate would disappear to give me enough time to break this woman. In cases like this, a cabin mate would hang out in the crew bar until my time was up. We normally gave each other two hours.

As we both entered the cabin, we started to take full advantage of our privacy. I turned the music on then gently held her hand and asked her for a dance. As she approached me, I reached out and turned the music down low. She wrapped her arms around my neck. I held her around her waist, and suddenly I got very aggressive and braced her up against the wall. Out of nowhere we began to kiss each other. Unexpectedly, there was a knocking on my door. "Bad timing," I said. I checked it out, and it was my cabin mate returning to pick something up. After a while, I left her to get some ice. I ran into the fire patrol man. I did not fear him because he did not know that I had a girl inside my cabin. As I reentered the cabin, she was waiting for me with a big surprise. I noticed the light was off. I felt for the switch and hit the light. The lady was undressed in my bed under the blanket waiting for me. What else was there to do but turn off the light?

A single lady cruised for many reasons. She might have been seeking a new man in her life, whether she was single or not. Some girls cruised just to have fun. Either the guys were attractive or not; only some weren't that picky. The type of girl I loved was the one who needed her home problem to be taken care of. She needed attention, the kind of home care she was not receiving.

Chapter-10

The period of one year caught me on board, and it was time to go on vacation. I flew home for four months where I enjoyed my stay to the max. Returning to work, I had to retake my medical exam. I happened to ride the same ship one more time. This time things were really getting out of hand. I was changed from snack steward to dishwasher. Now I was back in my water booth and stripe uniform for the second time. I had a talk with the kitchen steward and asked why my position was changed. He did not tell me straightforward what the true position was, but I just read between the lines. I knew all along that this oriental gay assistant food and beverage manager definitely did not favor me. I was glad for the distance between us, at least that's what I thought. This lowlife was still bothering me, trying to have me dismissed without a cause. This was the first time in my life that my heart became corrupted and devious, to kill and kill again. As soon as I reached the United States port, I sought a hand gun off the street; unfortunately, I could not raise one with a silencer. So I waited until the ship changed route to Puerto Rico. Down there I inquired of some of the prostitutes about getting a hand gun, and they asked me when I needed it.

I answered, "It is an emergency."

The prostitute said, "I know a place. Let me take you."

There was a taxi coming. I turned and looked as I put my right foot forward with the intention to stop the cab. I intentionally changed my mind. "Why don't I use her?" I said to myself. The taxi passed without stopping. "Okay," I said to her. "Let's sit down, and I will tell you what I am going to do. I personally will take care of you. It will work out the same as if we were together in a hotel room." I gave her fifty dollars.

She said, "Why so much?"

I said, "No problem. Don't worry; there is plenty where this comes from. Tonight's plans have been postponed. Tomorrow I want you to check out these guys for me, ask them the price for a nine millimeter with an extension clip. I am willing to pay the cost." I wanted to make sure this prostitute and I became good friends. That way, she would have to think twice before ripping me off. "Do you care to join me for a short drink?" I asked.

"Yeah," she answered. We crossed the street then entered the bar. This bar in the early days was right on the main street across from the ship. All the men inside were seamen. Some were from the same ship as me, and some were from another cruise line. Some who knew me well still hold on to their opinion that I fixed the prostitute that night. Every man was entitled to his own opinion. My main objective at the moment was to get the prostitute to bring me the tool I required. I became so impatient. "This guy must go down, and I mean now. He has but a short time to live because racism, discrimination, homosexuality, corruption, partiality, and nonhuman relations must come to an end tonight." The mentally strain took me on a road of no return. I became a murderer confused. I had to kill to ease this evil tension that possessed me totally. It burned my heart to know that this insane, brain-damaged slave driver had another night to live. It grieved me to my heart to know that I had to wait another full week before I heard from the prostitute about the situation. Before I made it back to the States, I received a yellow warning for the first time. This warning was spitefully given to me by the assistant food and beverage manager, the gay man. It stated that I was not complying with company rules and regulations; I was rude to the head of the department; noted misconduct; and I was late for work. It was the kitchen steward who brought me the yellow warning to sign. I asked him who gave it to him. He said the assistant food and beverage manager did.

"Let me explain something to you, then after I am finished, look me straight in the eyes and tell me to sign it if you really understand what I tell you. I am an excellent waiter. Back home, when people come from all over the world to our little island, who do you think serves them? It is us. We are the ones with the proper skills and experience that treat and show them good courtesy. When I came here, I learned that someone in the main office stated that they only wanted a European atmosphere in the dining room. Since I was rejected from the restaurant, I never tried to make it a big issue. You've known me a long time too. I just do my job, but the senseless piece of human waste cannot get me to be gay like him; for that reason, he keeps on pressuring me day by day. I want you to tell me now, can I be in my normal sense and be polite to this clown?"

"As far as I can see, the problem is not yours. Tell you what," he said, "let me have a word with the food and beverage manager, then I will get back to you."

"Okay, yes," I answered. Early the next morning, most of the crew was up getting the ship ready for the public health inspection. I saw the kitchen steward and called to him, "Hey B.J., what is up?"

B.J. answered, "I talked to the boss last night, and he said he knew where the problem is coming from, so the yellow slip was ripped up. Just do your job and don't pay that gay any mind." After a period of time, B.J. left the cruise line because his girlfriend wanted him to get off the ship. It broke my heart to hear B.J. was shot by some woman. I didn't know why until now. There was no kitchen steward that could compare to B.J.

As soon as the ship was cleared by the United States customs, I went browsing for the kind of weapon I would like to use to execute this gay man. That day I also purchased a Rambo knife in case the bloody gun stuck on me. My only hope and dream was on Puerto Rico.

In one week I was back in Puerto Rico again. I waited until it was nightfall before I left the ship. I knew the exact place to meet the prostitute. She had better be there; she was getting paid to be there. I used a taxi that night to drive around the block and check out the back. I passed the prostitute once then picked her up. I got off at a nearby hotel where I could talk privately. As a good sport, I paid her for the hotel time, which was twenty dollars.

"Okay," I said. "Let's go have a drink." I had one drink and said good night to her.

Immediately she said, "You going back to the ship?"

"Yes, right now."

"What about the deal?" she asked.

"Forget it," I said. These guys were such complete idiots, asking me to come over the hill of no return. Maybe these gang members believed that I might be some undercover agent. How senseless it was to invite me, a stranger, into their secret hiding place. They didn't know anything about me. The only contact that we had was through the prostitute. Once I reached over the hill, what made the prostitute think I might walk out alive?

I went back to the cabin, jumped straight up on my top bunk, lay on my back looking up to the ceiling, and started to reconstruct my idea all over. I could have lost my own life that night by trying to find a way to take another's. Self-rehabilitation was the only good thing that really happened to me.

The next morning while I was on duty, I ran into gay boy. Because the good side in me overcame the evil, I said hello first. He looked at me with surprise and smiled. It was a pity he did not know I just gave him a second chance to live, like I gave myself. We still didn't talk much, but at least the killer instinct was over.

Chapter-11

Our working schedule was another facture that I studied very carefully. The normal working hours, which were ten hours a day, were simply too much. Up to the time of my retirement, we did not have any union, so we had no rights. On several occasions, we ended up working more than ten hours per day, such as fourteen hours. The time frame that was set for our regular duty was inconvenient for our lunch time. Things were better. It used to be fun working with the good companies; now no more than three of these companies were in existence, but they were still cheap. I remembered long before the new contract came into circulation, working was less than ten hours per day. Cooks, cleaners, snack stewards, actually every department, received a case of beer and a case of Coke after every cruise. Plus we the snack stewards used to receive overtime to keep our pockets warm until payday came. Bonuses were paid every month to some men—one from each department, sometimes more. The captain and hotel manager would come down with the photographer. We would take pictures together while they handed us our bonuses and congratulated us for doing an outstanding job. It only took one cruise line to make one cheap move, and from this cheap move, that line would save more money and start to increase their fleet with modern ships. To do so, all salaries would be cut from the top to the very bottom—benefit cuts at certain percentages, no bonuses or overtime. I remember every week they gave the crew free sodas. Vacation pay was very good but not anymore. The quality of product was cut in all aspects. Sometimes one man ended up doing two men's jobs. Everything on board simply looked cheaper and tasted cheaper.

The difference depends on which department you worked in. It was difficult to sit and enjoy your meal like a normal decent person. Time was always against us. We had to eat and run up the stairs. Sometimes the main dining room schedule was set for lunch at twelve noon. The crew mess lunch was set for eleven thirty. All dining room personnel had to report at eleven forty-five. On duty they only had fifteen minutes to eat. Sometimes the lunch line was long and moving slow. You either ate and ran, or you sat down and enjoyed your lunch and paid the consequences later for being late. You would rarely see a cook in the crew mess eating because usually you would find them finger licking all the time. Plus a couple of them would cook their native dishes. Other departments did not experience this problem. When I was a snack steward, we used to help ourselves to burgers and hot dogs. As a dishwasher in the snack pantry, I relaxed on a full lunch break.

The bakers started out between four and five in the morning. They baked fresh Danish pastries and bread rolls for breakfast. The pastry shop never closed. A night man came on duty after dinner was done, and preparation was done for the next day's menu. You had the night dining room cleaner come in too. He vacuumed and spot-checked to make sure the restaurant was ready and presentable. On rotation, the waiters and busboys put in extra hours working the midnight buffet from twelve midnight to one thirty in the morning. The hotel cleaners were many; there was a night shift and a day shift. Whether it was night or day, one set of hotel cleaners would clean the passenger areas, and the other would clean the crew areas. Fire patrol worked right around the clock.

After I took my second vacation and came back, I went back to the pool café to work as a snack steward. At least I got rid of the water boots and the thick striped uniform again. The boys were happy to see me, and I was pleased to learn that the little gay assistant was transferred to another ship. The food and beverage manager that we now had was from the Caribbean. It looked like my life on board for the first time was going to be an easy one. I knew from birth that most Caribbean people were friendly and produced excellent human relationships amongst all nationalities. I met with the new food and beverage assistant. He looked like the kind of person everybody would get along with. First, he was a family man. Secondly, he spoke to us with respect, and third, he did not pressure us on the job. Not just because he was nice, we still came to work on time and did our job. The route we were sailing was perfect: Haiti, Puerto Rico, and St. Thomas, Virgin Island. Things became different now. Our lives became pleasurable. The pressure that this system provided toward the Caribbean man was not so tormented, again because of the new assistant we had on our side.

Arriving in Haiti for the first time, I was looking forward to enjoying myself. In every country, one would see poverty, but I saw it more here. Most of the prostitutes you would find in the day club came from across the border, and that was very surprising to me. We found good girls who were looking for good men on the beach, in the water, and in the bushes. Either they were having sex or not. I did not know; I was not a peeping tom. I saw bushes shaking all over the place. I did not know if it was man or beast.

I met a nice girl. She worked as a dentist's assistant. We had been going for a good while. She asked me for a picture of myself. I gave her one. I did not notice that the picture had disappeared. Inquisitive of me, I was searching through her things one day while she was in the shower. Suddenly I picked up this little basket and opened it. There was my picture all torn up and covered with some smelly powder. She was surprised and frightened. With a shout, she said, "Don't open it." From the look of everything, I knew it was voodoo.

I went out back and burned the basket. I turned to her and said, "A nice-looking girl like you who looks to be so respectable, why are you doing this madness?"

"Why?" she answered. "I do not want any other girl to take you away from me."

I said, "Baby, you went to the wrong voodoo man. Tell him things did not work out for you, and you would like your money back. Goodbye."

I heard that the head cooks were giving away food to the girls on the island. No wonder it was much easier for them to find a girlfriend than us. The section of the island where the captain dropped the ship anchor was nicely kept for the passengers and crew. This beautiful beach and its facilities only had two large restaurants that carried no closed doors or windows. A kitchen was provided for serving only. No major cooking was done over on the island. We used one special tender at all times to transport food from the ship to shore. As soon as the tender stopped, we would unload then reload to a truck waiting for us. Because the kitchen was three blocks from the loading dock, it was much easier for a transport to drop it off than to move it with manpower. Flies also was one of our biggest problems. Drinking water we would bring from the ship to the shore. We used it to mix lemonade and different refreshing drinks. The presence of the island security force could be seen, for what reason I could not say. I was told that these policemen were quick to shoot.

On the other side of the island, it was impossible to walk through the rock to reach the girls' section. For this reason, the fishermen would use their boats as taxis to take all the crew members who were interested to go over. Whenever a cruise ship was in, the fishermen did not go fishing that day. This side of the beach did not carry a platform for the crew to walk off the boat. The boat taxi came in very fast just to get the boat far as possible to dry land. The crew would jump off the boat to escape water from getting into their shoes. A small bar that only sold beer and plenty of young girls were there, and the cost for one was cheap. There was a certain set of men from the ship who were paying bigger tips than the others, and this really caused a problem. The next week when we returned to the same beach, by chance if you reached a girl before the big tipper, you would have to pay a bigger tip or else she was going to wait for the same guy who had tipped her generously last week. Finally the word got around, and the rest of the girls raised the price on all the crew members. It was a grand day as the guys repeatedly explained it; up to three girls for the day. Some crew members used condoms, while some didn't. Some would experience a clean girl that day. Unfortunately for some, they didn't. They would lie about it, saying they only went for a drink not to get involved with girls, but the truth always revealed the guilty ones. Two to three days after, I made it a point of my duty to pass by the sick bay. One by one I would notice certain crew members paying the doctor's office a visit. Normally now crew members can pick up their condoms at the bell desk before getting off at any port. Crew members who decided to keep their clap a secret would wait for the arrival into the United States port, or they would wait patiently until they returned to a Caribbean island.

As months passed by, the news hit the head office in the States that the working chef was giving away food to the women on the island, but it was not as strong as it sounds. The working chef may have been doing so, but I never saw him in the act. But in Haiti, anything goes. I later learned that the chef turner and the working chef were not drinking the same tea. The chef turner was jealous of the working chef's position. The only way to get rid of the working chef was to inform our big boss personally of who was the concessionaire. All unconcerned one day when everybody thought it was peaceful and safe during the lunch hour, you could find men on duty goofing off and finally ending up somewhere else on the island. You had men somewhere in the kitchen relaxing and enjoying a cold beer. I agreed that the island was hot, but in a few more minutes this little section of the island would get hotter than we knew.

The big boss flew in from the States early in the morning undercover. The office knew nothing of his presence, neither did any personnel on board know of his arrival. The big boss waited until noon when the island got busy. In the clothing he wore, no one was able to identify him. He was easily a millionaire but was dressed up like an ordinary working-class man. The big boss sat down under a tree where he could see the kitchen and all its movements. He was watching and waiting to prove for himself if what he heard was true. He definitely came to dismiss all whom he caught giving away his food. By accident one of the crew recognized the big boss and pretended not to blow his cover. But he circled back and broke the news. The food and beverage manager could not believe his eyes; he became nervous. The working chef was running up and down as if he saw a ghost. Some of the cooks quietly removed all the beer from the cooler and hid them. Everyone was panicked. Food that had been wrapped up in plastic and foil was now unwrapped and put aside as if it was a standby for a backup. All the guys that goofed off heard the shocking news and then re-entered their positions. It was best for them not to be recognized if they intended to keep their jobs. There was silence between the men as they were working at their best. As I stood there taking notes, I didn't really believe the passengers noticed the big difference around them or with the service. Well, since they did not catch it, nobody threw it. The big boss was upset and still not speaking with the working chef, after lunch was over and we all started to break down the line. The big boss made sure every leftover went back on the truck. Some of the men offered him a ride in the front just because he was our boss. He said, "No, I will stay in the back with the food." As he attempted to climb up the back of the truck, we all started to laugh because it seemed to us that this man had never climbed up a truck from the day he was born. Anyway, some of the guys helped him up the truck. Still he was not speaking to anyone. When the truck reached the loading dock, we had to help him down again because he was big and fat. That's why climbing was a problem for him. It was this day that I learned how serious one should take money or any business. I was not displeased with this man. Neither was I feeling uncomfortable working in his presence because I normally did my job. I had no fear of man. This day truly was the first time I witnessed all the crew members tune in together and unload the truck, and it was the fastest I had ever seen the boat reload without any hesitation. The last tender for passengers was about to leave when the food and beverage manager asked the big boss to ride with the passengers again. The answer was, "No, I want to ride with the food if you don't mind."

"I don't," answered the food and beverage manager. The boat was packed. Some crew members had to ride on top. The big boss couldn't care less where anyone wanted to ride once he saw that his food left the island and none of it stayed behind. He sat on top of the food container, proceeding across to the ship. The big boss did not try to stand up; it took good balance to do so when the water was a bit choppy. If he attempted to move, for sure a fall was coming his way. I had no respect for him. As we moved along the starboard side, two men were in position to tie the rope of the tender. Now it was time to unload, and I just couldn't believe my eyes when the big boss started to help us unload the food. I was kind of pleased to see that, because most management on board did not lift a finger. Our boss was the last person to leave the tender, just to make sure all food was returned to the kitchen. In any business, as soon as the owner or president turned his back, in came the slackness again, so flying down to prove a point was a waste of time.

Chapter-12

The system that I had to live with was now in the past. This was not the system I had learned in the Caribbean, where civilized people dwelled with only one love and equality for all. This system promoted mental slavery and corruption. This system promoted segregation, nonhuman relations, drugs, discrimination, gambling, stealing, prostitution, and lots more. I was educated by the older crew members from the Caribbean all about this system, a system that provided less for us and more for the Europeans. In the early eighties, I personally knew of two cruise lines that employed a lot of Caribbean men. Until this day, Caribbean men held big position without working in the utility department for five to ten years. It was way below standard to provide a system where Caribbean salaries were under four hundred dollars per month while the European boys went straight to the dining room where the least they could make was five hundred dollars per week. In every port, the dining room staff would go out to find good entertainment, spend their money foolishly, and come back just to show off to us guys. They knew that we the utility men couldn't afford it. Because of this system, some men from the Caribbean were forced unwillingly and reluctantly to do drugs just to support their families and personal needs. Because of this system, women with low salaries were forced unwillingly and reluctantly to transport drugs since they were hardly ever searched by customs and police. It was a risk they would have to take to provide for their necessities. This system promoted thieves because of the low monthly salary, and passengers were the ones who ended up being the victims. This system was created to oppress the weak and the needy. This was a system from long ago, ignorantly planned by a group of unintelligent and uncivilized people. This system could not be abolished until jointly corrupted leaders were infiltrated.

For many years, leaders in the Western Hemisphere closed their eyes intentionally or were naturally blind to certain cruise lines that used our port. I personally experienced that Caribbean men were undermined and disliked and faced daily discomfort. The only job that seemed fit for us by these people with no morals or integrity was a utility position. The positions within the utility department were dishwasher, pot washer, day cleaner, garbage man, and many more. It was much easier for us Caribbean men to get a job as a utility bar waiter or cook than a dining room waiter, where the most money could be made. Any Caribbean man with the ambition that caused him to try too hard for the dining room was considered to be a troublemaker. Too much perseverance could cause management to dislike you. Once a crew member was a utility worker and his job was looked upon as an outstanding performance, actually everybody would like him. This system promoted gambling and death. On board, all the gamblers would get together and select whose cabin should be used as their private casino. Every night after duty, the private casino members would meet each other at the hideout. It was hard to recognize that illegal gambling was being conducted on board.

It all happened one night that one of the guys hit another in the face over the gambling table. The individual that received the blow replied, "No man hits me and lives." Peacefully he left the private casino for a short walk to his cabin and back. It was surprising to the others when he returned with a hand gun. Pitifully, Mr. Chuck was asking for his life to be spared. No mercy was shown. There was a big bang to the side of the head, and he died on the spot. The killer then walked back to his cabin and put the hand gun on top of his television set and waited for the authorities on board to come and arrest him. This incident took place in international waters. He was flown to a destination where the ship was registered and stood trial in that country. He was found guilty and sentenced to serve at least twenty years in prison because of the system.

Many Caribbean men were in jail in so many different countries. Because of this system, the homosexual supervisor on board gave the Caribbean men the most problems without the knowledge of the main office on shore side. There were thousands of ex-Caribbean seamen who could testify to this as a fact. Because of this corrupted system, it took years of kissing ass, arguments, promises, and humiliation before any pity was shown to me, to work in the dining room as a waiter. When foreigners visited our island, they always received a warm welcome from us. According to my memory, I kept on asking the food and beverage manager to give me a chance so I could make some money. His evil reply was that I needed at least four references before he could help me. I looked at him. I knew it was a waste of time talking to this idiot.

Months later, I saw someone from the main office pay us a visit on board. He looked like someone with dignity. "Good morning, sir," I said to him.

He replied, "Morning to you."

I said, "Sir, can you spare me a moment of your time please?"

"Certainly. What can I do for you?"

"I am experiencing some difficulties with both shore side and on board. I do not want it to sound too strong."

"Like what?" he asked. I explained everything to him clearly in order for him to understand me. His reply to me was, "I will take care of this."

I was surprised that in less than a month, one afternoon an officer shamefully came to me like a dog wagging his tail. He could hardly look me in the face, knowing that I was about to break through a system that he firmly supported. He called me by name and told me that on the next cruise, I would be going to work as a busboy. I was not that happy when he told me because I knew my road was going to be a rough and rocky one.

First, I was not greeted warmly like I saw it done with the European boys. I felt like a complete stranger. The five, more or less, Caribbean waiters that I saw still made me feel out of place with the total of a little over a hundred dining room personnel. Still, I could hardly see us. It was like we were lost in a crowd. The dining room opened at 6 PM that evening for the first seating. The dining room manager's meeting that started at five fifteen had to end no later than five forty-five so that every waiter and busboy would have enough time to prepare their stations. When I reached my station that evening, I realized that it was a very small station for a man of my experience. It was two tables that carried nine passengers each—a total of eighteen passengers for the week. That was outrageous. I took it with a smile because it was my first cruise as a busboy. I thought maybe they wanted to watch my performance. The dining room management watched me intently on my first night as if I were a criminal. My experience and boldness took me through the night. With such a small station and with some passengers paying less, I barely made two hundred dollars that week, and this brain-damaged maitre d' kept me on the same two tables for a month. I never asked him for a bigger station like the boys from Europe. If I made that approach, for sure in his report he would have stated that I was arguing with him. I carefully learned about this system. Either the European boys asked for a bigger station or they always received the large ones. I was told they only needed a European atmosphere in the dining room, and the reason why we the Caribbean boys were in the dining room was only to dance the babaloo dance every Caribbean night, which was similar to a limbo dance. Any night that a Caribbean waiter could not dance, whatever the reason, the head waiters and maitre d' would pull a long face.

This system also could influence any weaklings definitely to become homicidal. It also converted a lot of law-abiding crew members into drug dealers. This corruption was a dream that I wanted to see put to an end by all Caribbean heads of government for the future of our young men who dreamed of traveling by sea and making it their career. As long as the cruise lines continued to sail and visit our beautiful island, we should have gotten the opportunity to share the dining room with equal rights. Such a system should have been deeply investigated by every ex-seaman. If this system continued to live, the future of a far-distant country would advance over us. In some countries up east, only the men from those areas could work on such lines, as I remember clearly without any doubt, because I knew these guys. We talked about the discrimination that we all had to work under. Working with a concessionaire that had concessions on many different lines, we found out that not all the lines are in favor of us Caribbean men working inside the dining room as waiters.

There was a waiter from Jamaica. He learned of another cruise line that used the Montego Bay free port as their main terminal for six months out of the year. Since this port was closer to his home, he asked the main office for a transfer. He flew over one morning to the Montego Bay international airport, where he would join the ship in his own country. Along with him were some other guys from different countries. Fortunately, he was the first Caribbean waiter to get the opportunity to see his family once a week. It was a dream come true. The management on board this ship certainly was a part of a corrupted organization that opposed Caribbean men in the dining room. This Jamaican waiter signed on that morning. It was humiliating to learn from him that he signed off the same day in Montego Bay because of their idiotic policy. It hurt to know that he was accompanied by the corporate manager for the dining room whose office was on shore side. He was to make sure that when immigration asked the Jamaican waiter for the reason he was not sailing the answer would be there was no space available.

This same line sailed out of Montreal, Canada, on a one-week cruise to Manhattan, New York. Four of us Caribbean men flew into Montreal to join the vessel. Everything was going fine until the last day at sea. The maitre d' called all four of us into his office and explained that it was the company's policy that was against using us in their dining room. So upon arrival in New York, we four would be signing off. Because of this, all the cooks and utility workers were planning a strike. They started out with a go-slow. When the food and beverage manager heard about this, he came down and asked them to return to their duties. They did return with a protest.

Chapter-13

Side jobs were extra duties without pay. Every dining room worker on board had a side job he was in charge of. Forgetting to do your duty was a much more serious offense than giving bad service to the passengers because not all passengers could recognize sloppy service. When one of us neglected or forgot to do our side job, it instantly became known. Because each man depended on the other, it was like teamwork. Each duty was very important. For example, one waiter would feed the maitre d' and the head waiters every night. It was very rare that they would request breakfast or lunch. When the restaurant service was finished, the maitre d' and the head waiter would sit down with the expectation that their hot meal was about ready to be served. If the waiter forgot to put in the order, this would be a very big disappointment for them. It is a fact, because I knew the nature of these men. There was another waiter who was in charge of tablecloths. His duty was to ensure that the tablecloths were available for setting up and to change them between seatings. The same goes for the waiter who was in charge of napkins. We had four to six waiters who were in charge of salt and pepper, sugar, oil, and vinegar, etc. If passengers did not have these items during the service, these men would answer to the maitre d'. Seriously, one waiter was in charge of the curtain along the windows, to close and open it on occasion. Another was in charge of extra silver because there were times when some tables were short, and the waiter who was assigned to those tables had to find the silver man in order for him to make a full setup. There was another waiter whose side job was to keep the mirror clean. This extra duty I considered to be one of the toughest because every second, someone would touch the mirror with his or her hand, both passengers and crew members. When passing through the dining room, the hotel manager and the food and beverage manager loved to spot-check this mirror. Not once would it ever occur to them that someone might have just touched the mirror. Another waiter was in charge of keeping the dining room manager's office clean. He liked to snoop around the paperwork when cleaning, and before the day was out, all the dining room personnel would know ahead of all the other crew members on board what the company's plans were. My side job was the carpet. I had to check for spots, and this was the toughest mainly because I was a new boy. The carpet never stayed clean. At any time there was always someone making a spill. When it was not the passengers, it was the crew. On the captain's inspection morning, I had to check the whole dining room for spots or stains with a bucket of hot water, a brush, and some bleach so that the carpet would look presentable. Whatever was one's extra duty, it was vital to everyone and the company that it was done. Also, at the end of the three-month period, the maitre d' would fill out an evaluation form on all dining room workers' performances then give it to us to read and sign. Whether you agreed to sign it or not, this was his judgment.

Chapter-14

Spitting on others on the job was what most dining room management did best, and they enjoyed doing so. Their outward appearance was in the form of a man, but inward they occupied the mind of an idle child and were very much idiotic. On board, every European management's top priority was that their countrymen received the best treatment. Once a group or full charter arrived, the maitre d's special men would be assigned to the largest station. It was plain to see, but nobody was foolish enough to complain on the dining room manager because officers were friends, and when they sat down together eating or drinking, every crew member's name reached the surface. I often wondered what sense it made to complain about an officer, whenever a waiter tried to comply with company policy. The dining room manager could not find a real reason to penalize him, but because of a dislike, he would use his confederate to approach you and start talking bad things about him. If good intellect failed to guide you through such an uncivilized plot, you would be miserable for the rest of your life working with him.

On the first night of every cruise, confusion took full control of the dining room. Passengers began to get picky searching for the best table. Some passengers who belonged to a group of six or ten would seek a table to accommodate their party. There were those who were looking for a table of two, which was limited. Normally, couples would rush to catch a window table. Meanwhile, other people were moving around the dining room looking for friends they chose to sit with. There were passengers who continued to move from table to table, especially the younger ones; they were looking forward to sitting with their age group. When all passengers were seated and had placed their orders, then calmness would take its course. The behavior of some passengers only told us on board that quality and class did not walk their way at the time of birth. The men would pass their feet over the backrest of the chair to sit. They would get ice and water from their water glasses with a teaspoon to throw water at each other around the table. The chairs they sat on would be used to block other waiters and passengers. Frequently, waiters had to excuse themselves when approaching to take their order. We were disregarded. The impression I gathered was that most likely these passengers had serious problems dining out. They also had a way of pushing a waiter to anger. One passenger would ask you for orange juice. When the waiter returned, the other also asked for the same thing. As a waiter, I made sure to ask the whole table if anyone else cared for some juice, and they all would say no. After I made my second round to the table, someone would say, "Sorry, I have changed my mind. I think I will have an apple juice too," and they all would start to laugh. So I did what most waiters would have done. For the last person to ask for juice, I would stay a little longer in the juice station just to let him wait. As I showed up, they would call me by name and say, "What took you so long? We were just about to send out a search party to look for you." So I would play a big liar and say, "Sorry, the juice ran out, and I had to wait for the buffet runner to remix it."

Anyway at the end of the cruise, there were waiters who became most fortunate, and it all added up to their performance. Knowing that the cruise was prepaid, very few passengers would notice the long hours and how hard we worked, even though some waiters dropped the service standard. Some passengers were satisfied with the entire cruise and tipped their waiters again. Tipping in general was unpredictable. We knew that our pay stated fifty dollars per month and the only good way to make some serious money was for people to cruise a lot, and only if they could afford it. If any individual saved for a whole year, he could come up with at least two thousand dollars for a ticket and could afford to tip. Passengers with credit cards certainly would tip because they carried extra money on them. A big family was likely to tip less. Honeymooners and couples were excellent tippers. A family with too many kids normally tipped less. A person who was in charge of a group of handicapped passengers or a single handicapped person always tipped excellent with the experience that I have had on board. No European waiters liked to serve handicapped passengers on their tables. The passengers who could not afford to tip felt embarrassed to inform their waiters, which was not the best thing to do. Most waiters appreciated being told there was no tip; at least they expected that. All tips had to be paid on the last night of the cruise. There was a tip guide inside their rooms for passengers who cruised for the first time. These people would normally tip on the last night, but if they sat with repeaters, they would be informed by them that it was better to tip on the embarkation morning because once most waiters received their tips on the last night, the service would not be the same in the morning. Many passengers complained about the last morning's service.

My experience on board with this kind of attitude amongst waiters and busboys was that every dining room worker would like to receive his envelope on the last night of the cruise and not in the morning. If they doubted that any passenger around the table would not pay on this last night of the cruise, the envelope that they had received from the other tables would be placed in their front breast pocket so that the other passengers would notice that it was tipping time. Also, all envelopes were marked by the waiters and the busboys with our secret codes. As soon as the service was over and the dining room was empty, all the waiters and busboys would sit down and check their envelops carefully one by one. It would be a big loss if any envelope was overlooked and thrown in the garbage. Any envelope that came up short in tips could be easily identified. Immediately we could tell which one of the passengers tipped us cheaply. Because of this, the last morning breakfast was already planned by waiters and busboys overnight to produce poor service on the embarkation morning. Also, these were the type of people that made complaints about the service. A smart waiter knew perfectly well when a passenger did not intend to pay. They normally told us on the last night, "Sorry, we did not receive any envelope in our cabin." And they would ask us the same question every cruise: "Are you going to be here in the morning?" Some waiters would answer no so they would go to their cabin

and return with the envelopes right away. A few passengers would keep their promise and bring their envelopes on the last morning. It was a wise move, but still there was a possibility for a lesser tip when they paid in the morning. If the complete table agreed to pay less because of the waiter's performance, it only took one passenger to collect the envelopes from the others and place them all in the center of the table. By doing so, neither busboy nor waiter could identify who paid the cheapest. Most passengers preferred to deliver their envelopes at the last moment when they finished their breakfast and were leaving the table, because waiters and busboys normally gave them a dirty look after realizing that their tip was short, so at the last moment, they would not have to take such looks and feel embarrassed.

During the last dinner on every cruise line, we performed in a parade for our passengers. Some of us were hopeless concerning our tips once we joined that line to sing. We felt anxious and rushed the last night's parade because the moment of truth was about to break loose. While we sang "America the Beautiful" at this special moment, a few passengers whom I believed to be patriotic. We evidently beheld them with our eyes as they left the table to avoid tipping us. We certainly were not stupid enough to break a parade line to chase some cheap person for money. Most certainly, the runaway faces wouldn't be showing up for breakfast on the embarkation morning because they lacked money. There were a few understanding passengers who separated and sealed all tips from the first night because hitting the casino, over-shopping, or playing expensively could terminate one's financial support before the cruise came to an end.

I clearly remembered four people who were assigned to my table. There was one African-American young couple, and the other two men were European American cruising together. These two men partially deceived me. I thought they were rich after ordering from the wine steward a bottle of Dom Perignon. On top of that, they were purposely showing off for the African-American couple. Their behavior was like real millionaires, laughing loud just to get other passengers' attention. Personally, I disregarded other passengers when I was serving my tables because they came first. It was my passengers who paid me on the last night, not the others. Before I could serve the main course, the wine steward brought another bottle of Dom Perignon. It was strange to me that the couple sitting across from them was not offered a drink. They were two selfish rich men.

The next night was the captain's cocktail party, and after the party was over, everybody headed straight for the dining room all dressed up in their expensive attire. During every captain's dinner, passengers would order wine or champagne to go along with the items they ordered from the menu. That night, I realized the African-American couple was moved by the head waiter to another table. As the two men approached my table, I was embarrassed by the way things turned around so quickly. They were wearing jeans and sneakers, the same set of clothing they wore on the first night. Now I knew my dream for a big tip at the end of the cruise was in vain. These two hillbillies were drinking beer on the second night. They could not afford to buy a glass of wine with their dinner. At the end of the cruise, they only tipped me for one person instead of two.

The other experience that I had involved two families of four that occupied a table of eight. They never gave me their envelope on the last night after dinner. They left the restaurant without saying thank you or "I will see you in the morning." Such cheap behavior forced me to disregard them, because they showed no regard for the one person whose responsibility it was to take good care of them while being at home away from home. On embarkation morning, all eight passengers showed up for breakfast. I did not show them a long face because of my professional training I received in training school. I still held on to some faith, hoping that I might get lucky. After breakfast was over, the ladies and kids left the table without tipping. Suspicious from the night before, I pulled my busboy aside and told him that in the morning both of us should leave the station at the same time. He asked me why. "To prove a point," I told him. As we attempted to leave together, the two men at our table believed we were leaving. Both men tried to run for it. Suddenly we doubled back very fast to prove to my busboy that I was right about them. I said, "Surprise, we are back." They both sat down. Knowing that they wanted to leave, I stood in my station like a security guard punishing them, looking straight into their eyes. They could hardly look back at me, suspecting that I knew their plan. Shamefully the first man got up and handed me his envelope. He left without shaking my hand. Seconds after, the other gentleman got up. He said nothing and gave me nothing.

Passengers smartly asked waiters personal questions. Receiving your tip sometimes depended on how you answered their questions. Once a passenger got the impression that a waiter was better off than he or she was, the tipping on the last night would be cut in half or less than half. Passengers normally asked me where I was from, if I had my own home, if I was married, if I had a family, how many there were in my family, how old the kids were, what kind of school they attended, if I owned a car, if yes they would ask what type, what I did while on vacation, if I worked or not while I was on vacation, how long I had worked with the cruise line, what my plans were when I retired, how much longer I planned to work on the ship, what my wife did for herself, and many more personal questions. After studying these people closely and what the full meanings of these questions were, most waiters came up with a master plan and were well prepared for them. For instance, he might go to an undeveloped country to take a picture of naked children or a child and pretend that he is the real father, and on top of that, we as waiters had to be full of convincing speech. By being a perfect liar, passengers would automatically feel sorry for us—like telling them that last month my house was burnt to the ground; telling them that our mother just died, and we had to go home at the end of the cruise; and especially telling about children, tell them anything bad like your kid had been poisoned and died last year. They liked you better when you told them you were from a poor family, and you were now working to help everybody. Everything a waiter or a busboy said he must remember so as not to contradict himself. Whenever a passenger asked questions, these would be the answers, and at the end of the cruise, as expected, your envelope was fatter.

Christian chartering on the ship meant harder work than ever. They only came to worship and eat. They were not gamblers, so the casino would be closed for the whole cruise; likewise, at the bar two wine stewards would stay on duty in case someone needed wine or a soft drink. Not everyone on board was holy, because by their fruit you could know them. Personally speaking, I was a hard believer when it came to European-American Christian practice. The place they spent most of their time was in the dining room for breakfast, lunch, and dinner. During their first evening on board, dinner was about to be served at 7 PM. The doors were open, and all the waiters had to escort passengers to their stations. If my station was the first to be full, that's how I would receive my pay. Plus, the service would advance ahead of the others, as the European waiters continued to call the passengers to be seated. It was in vain for some of Caribbean boys. Speaking for myself, the passengers passed me like I was not in existence. They all headed straight to the European tables. When most tables were full, not one single passenger sat in my station. I stepped aside so that none would recognize that the table they were about to sit around belonged to a Caribbean waiter. People sat in my station. Still it was not full yet, but I could see them looking around for menus. I still stayed out of sight until my tables were completely full. I then approached them with a pleasant smile and introduced myself. "Good evening, ladies and gentlemen. My name is John Doe, and I will be your waiter for the remainder of the cruise." I thought for a minute that they were all handicapped. Nobody had heard a word I just said. Without another word in English, I passed the menus around and explained a few details to them. Before I took their order, I suggested more than three items. I started to wonder what kind of Christian people they were. From the first moment, none was friendly enough to exchange a word with me. Generally on a charter cruise, passengers liked to behave like at a round robin. They sat at any table they pleased the next morning because it was a charter cruise. Breakfast was open seating. The people that sat with me the night before ignorantly were going to sit with a European waiter for breakfast. For the joke of it, I took the privilege of not lifting a straw that morning, purposely applying some pressure to my fellow waiters by standing in my station. As long as these Christian European-Americans saw me, I would enjoy myself doing nothing for the rest of the morning until lunchtime. Lunch turned out to be the same. Because of their behavior, I personally could not care less who they sat with. I was not the one with the attitude problem.

Once a waiter was possessed with an amount of insight professionally, he determined the type of service to be rendered. We engaged with people from all over the world, and depending on which country, state, or town they were from, it made a big difference in their behavior. When sitting at their assigned tables, there were two different types of cruisers that I knew of: ones were expensive and the others that were inexpensive. We with the proper insight studied these passengers very closely. A majority of the rich ones were old people mixed with middle-aged. Any young ones cruising were with parents or grandparents. This kind ate a lot, plus they give a lot of hard times. They were hard to please and very demanding, especially the very old ones. When a passenger was too old and sickly, his or her taste came and went. Even though what we served was fresh to them, it always carried a different flavor, and because of their misjudgment in taste, the item we served was always refused. Plus, some of them were very rude. Still, we had to treat them like babies. The older they were, the longer they took to give their order, and they took twice as long to finish their meal than a younger person. When it was not eye problems, it was nerves or loss of memory. The longer any passenger took to give his or her order, the longer the service was rendered, and these were the same people who always complained about the service. The passengers who were in their forties and fifties still had their sense of taste.

The inexpensive lines had travel agents who would recommend them to people who could not afford luxury cruises. I learned from other passengers that the only problem the inexpensive lines had was that they needed to improve on their food and the water. A passenger who was a hardworking person like a construction worker or a grave digger or any job that made a man sweat, his or her behavior was always better, and he or she was much easier to satisfy. We the waiters judged passengers by their appearance and their hygiene behavior, their personality and the type of conversation they liked to keep, and their table etiquette. We didn't care where in the world these people came from, it was our duty as waiters to determine the quality of service that should be served based on our professional experience, both in service and public relations. It took me several years to break my English standard of handing down prestige service. I couldn't make it. I later learned that I had to be a food carrier when serving these people, pretending to be a clown and playing dumber than your passenger. To hell with the service. This job was all about money, and the type of passenger we mostly carried did not like you if you looked smarter.

I realized that the dining room was like a circus; head waiters, waiters, and busboys planned tricks for their own assigned passengers as if the cruise line employed them as magicians. I was not a magician, but the fact still remained that if I couldn't make it, I had to play a clown for the clowns. As soon as the dining room was open for dinner, all waiters had to be in their assigned stations to greet their passengers with a smile, pull out their chairs, and open their napkins on their laps, then hand them the menu. A few waiters who believed they were movie stars were never present in their stations to have the honor of meeting, introducing, or seating their passengers. This was not service. Passengers sat themselves down and waited, wondering who was their waiter. Sometimes when the door was open, one station could take up to fifteen minutes before becoming completely full. During these extra minutes, some waiters used to go down to their cabins to take a drink for the road or a sniff of cocaine.

Service had now begun, and it was normal for us to introduce both ourselves and our busboys together. I enjoyed doing that for a very special reason. I evidently observed that Americans did not get along with each other, so I made sure that whenever introducing myself, I let my passengers be aware that I was a Caribbean boy, also my island and town, in order to have a perfect waiter-passenger relationship that I fought for every cruise. Some passengers liked fast service, while some liked it slow. It was very complicated to have old people sitting with younger ones. Waiters and busboys should have worked as a team regardless what country they were from. Other busboys of different nationalities hated working and taking orders from the Caribbean waiters that they were assigned to. Because of such protests, unfortunately the passengers did not receive the service that the company requires. For this reason, a few waiters normally ended up with a bad service record because of the busboy. Because of my professional flexibility, I was able to recognize when any of my passengers had a reading problem when handing them the menu. To avoid embarrassment, I professionally took the opportunity to explain the menu to them. At a fine restaurant on shore side, the service could be different. The service on board the ship that I had experience on could never reach the heights of perfection because of the dining room personnel on board. It was very painful to us, the older crew, when a new boy got promoted over us. After closely examining the operation, I realized that countrymen always helped their country man, and there are many old-timers who know the job. The rumor went around very fast that money makes the mail run. Once guys kept buying their way out, the quality of the service kept on deteriorating. Passengers constantly complained about cold food. Most of the time, this complaint cause through the kitchen and busboy with bigger station than they can handle. When I became a busboy, I had to serve drinks and coffee to every passenger in my station, and after the waiter served the appetizer, he left to pick up the soup. The old station should have been cleared before he returned. Sometimes I had two or three waiters I had to work with. If I was slow, when the waiter returned with the soup, he would have to clear the appetizer plates himself, and the next thing you knew, the soup got cold so fast because of the air conditioning. The same thing occurred to the main dishes. A waiter always depended on the busboy to clear all salad from the table, If any table was still unclear at the time of his return, the waiter would complain to the head waiter, and he would come over and give me a hard time. When I became a waiter, I didn't care how much I complained on my busboy; nobody would say a word to him because they were all countrymen. If a lousy busboy was assigned to my station, I proudly did his part so that the passengers could notice that, and at the end of the cruise, his tip would be less, and mine would be increased.

It was a regular practice for most of the dining room personnel to stay up late at night after the dining room service was over at 10:30 PM. You would find most of the crew linking up with each other, smoking some pot and partying. In the morning, because these guys were lacking sleep and had hangovers, not one of these guys would appreciate seeing their passengers' faces for breakfast until lunchtime. In such a state like this, none was in a service mood. In a case like this, if passengers should turn up for breakfast, the waiters seriously refused to smile, pull their chairs out, or open their napkins, which was a part of the service. The ones that smiled certainly did not smile from their heart.

There were some indications that some passengers would notice when they were on a cruise. This would help them to recognize if their waiters or busboys liked them or not. The words frequently used by busboys and waiters when they disliked their passengers were *mother f-----* and *son of a b-----*. They used words like these when passengers were approaching for breakfast, when these people were coming too early, when they couldn't sleep, or big babaloo,—the word *babaloo* in ship terminology means not good. Word like bastard, or may be water is in their bed. Every nationality used their own language. Some dining rooms created their own systems, like one team would come for breakfast in the morning while the other half slept in bed. This rotated every day. Some busboys would sleep in the morning because they worked the midnight buffet. Some waiters slept in the morning too—we called it lobster off—by convincing the passengers that the other items were better, but if you added it all up, this was not good for any company at all, because passengers always complained. The busboys and waiters were supposed to take care of the extra tables that belonged to the other busboys and waiters who were sleeping while their passengers were facing another team with an attitude. They only cared about their own passengers and not those of the sleeping team. If all passengers arrived, it became a problem. The sleeping team's passengers would not receive the full length of service, because at the end of the cruise the rating would not affect them but those who were sleeping. What really took place in the morning was that the busboy would serve his passengers coffee first whether the sleeping team's passengers were there before or not, and what hurt me most was that these boys could not care less about the other passengers. If a complaint reached the maitre d' about any one of these countrymen, he would talk smoothly with them, but if the complaint was directed to a Caribbean boy, he would confront him in a hostile manner. I for one did not support the lobster off, and thousands of passengers could testify that it is a fact, and hundreds of dining room personnel would say yes if they were investigated individually.

The dining room management normally said, "Gentlemen, remember to push the fish and the chicken, and the beef is good. Only on the Caribbean night will we serve half of a Florida lobster. The waiter that serves no lobster will sleep the next morning." When this system first started, a lot of waiters started to cheat the maitre d' who only checked the tickets we gave to the chef. If a waiter served one or two lobsters, he was going to write down an extra fish or lamb to get his morning off. It was a long time before the management found out that the waiters were cheating. This was not fair to passengers who traveled from far distances with the expectation of having Florida lobster for the first time in their entire lives. Mostly on the first night, passengers would ask me which night the lobster would be served. They also saw this lobster advertisement whenever the company was promoting the cruise. On the other hand, some passengers demanded lobster tail from us and they were determined to have lobster for dinner.

Chapter-15

I learned a lot about passengers, especially on the family cruise line. I have experienced passengers refusing to sit with each other. A table of six, eight, or ten could be assigned for two families. Very rarely would two families sit down at one time. Normally one sat before the other. On occasion when the second family approached the table, the presence of the first family was not accepted by them; therefore, they would turn away and ask for the maitre d', requesting a table change. Whatever that reason was I could not say, but from my experience, it could be for many reasons. Maybe the first family was not to their standard, or they simply needed to sit with a family whose kids were of the same age group. Before the second family sat down, the father especially would turn his back and immediately ask for the maitre d' to arrange for a different table because he definitely did not like this one. This man saw something that any blind man could have seen. Some families with kids did not have any table manners. First, the kids would start to play with all the utensils on the table, and once they started to touch these items that belonged to the second family, certainly they needed to be sanitized again. Secondly, the kids would carelessly turn over chocolate milk, iced tea, or fruit punch. And now the whole table would look like a pigsty. No one in their right mind would like to join them for a whole cruise. Most kids were rude, and the parents could hardly keep them under control. They moved from table to table disturbing other passengers. Once, when a waiter came out from the kitchen with fifteen to eighteen main courses, which I considered to be very heavy, out of nowhere I saw a little child run between the waiter's legs and cause him to be unbalanced. Next to him, passengers sat down peacefully enjoying their meal when suddenly plates with hot food came tumbling over their heads and down the backs of their suits, creating a big discomfort. If this passenger was a big babaloo and gave his waiter a difficult time, his waiter would feel pleased over the incident. Half the food served to the kids could be found beneath the table. For passengers who ate sloppily, it was a waste of time trying to provide neat service. There were times when a passenger sat down and his first movement was to push all silverware to the center of the table, Then during every course that was served, I would be asked by him which one of the utensils he should use.

During service hours, I was one of the last waiters to leave the kitchen, and the reason for this was that it was my natural common practice not to be involved with the rush that the majority of the waiters portrayed. Those who rushed during the main seating only tried to buy half an hour's idle time before the second seating started. Some waiters would have liked to take a break from their weary feet. Others would have liked to take a smoke, a drink, or recharge with some hard drugs, while some would like to go to the restroom. The second seating was normally slower, but on occasion you would find a few waiters rushing. Many of these passengers had no idea what excellent service was, and what I observed with these waiters while in their stations was that the only service they gave was holding conversations with their guests. What most passengers failed to notice was that their waiter always tried to take the order before they were ready. When you looked a waiter in his eye, especially when other passengers found it difficult to make up their mind what to select from the menu, you could definitely see that impatient look telling you to hurry up. You could notice how fast your waiter moved off when he was finished taking the order, like he was in the Indy 500. Unfortunately you might just have been the one to observe that your waiter brought to his side stand both appetizers and soup together. The soup would stay on top of the side stand until such passengers finished their appetizers. Thousands of passengers did observe these things, and hundreds of waiters and other crew members could testify to this.

Poor dining room management, poor waiters, and a low standard of service was what most European waiters and busboys produced. Consequently, a few people who did not experience excellent restaurant service would carelessly not note how sloppy their waiter performed. Once one person around the table liked this waiter, there was a possibility that the others would fall in love too. Passengers took a cruise for many reasons; only a few came to tie the knot. We had the honeymooners and those who came to celebrate anniversaries and birthdays. There were also those who cruised for family reunions. There were people who could not buy extension to life [sick], cruise with us to enjoy the last moment. Some came to find attention because back home nobody saw them and pampered them like we did. Some came to show off, not to receive and enjoy the service we provided. Some people repeated their cruise because of their previous waiter and the excellent service they had experienced. A few females would return on special occasions.

Chapter-16

After experiencing more than ten years on different cruise lines as an associate with many crew views, I have learned that the only two ways the cruise line could make a five-star rating was either the staff on board asked the passengers for a complete excellent markup or they simply professed to them their natural talent in providing the service expected on any cruise line. You found crew members asking passengers for an excellent mark or explaining how the procedure on the comment card worked. Just to achieve ten across the board was not a five-star line. Regardless how new or old a ship was, some line cabin stewards and waiters at the end of the cruise talked about the comment card to our passengers, which was soliciting. Without this compassion from the passengers, these lines would have been at the bottom of the list. The competition between lines was strong. Money had been spent consistently on advertising the company names and brochures, yet passengers still complained about the food and service. It was more complicated and pressuring for us waiters when working for a concessionaire instead of one owner concerning the rating. Companies that I knew ran the operation for themselves enforced that soliciting was against their rules, and when the crew was caught or reported begging for excellent ratings it was an immediate dismissal, which was the right system to work under. The quality of a company should be based upon the entire crew, on what they had to offer and how they offered it. It is stupid for a waiter and unfair for the passenger whose experience on board was not satisfactory in general to beg for excellent ratings; it was so embarrassing. I agreed that working for a concessionaire we waiters had no choice than to beg for excellent marks. To achieve the highest mark gave us the opportunity to obtain a big station. They say soliciting was against the rules, but the ratings had something to do with the company and the concessionaire. Whenever the rating went down, the dining room manager would state in his meeting, "Gentlemen, the rating is low this cruise. We have to keep it up above 9.89 or 2.94." Any figure below these was considered to be low. This simply means that the concessionaire's side was not doing well. Many others, including my self, were demoted from waiter to busboy because of low ratings we received from passengers. Normally the waiters made more money than the busboys did. Some waiters quit after a demotion from waiter to busboy. To keep our position as waiters, thousands of passengers that cruised would testify to the truth that on certain cruise lines we explained the comment card to them before asking for excellent marks. We did this because we needed money in our pocket. The strain and the stress with the station plus management on board was more than we could bear to achieve the heights of excellence.

Chapter-17

During the period I spent working together among several different nationalities, my main concern was to pay special attention to everyone's personal hygiene attitude. To begin with, most cooks in the kitchen did not carry a handkerchief or a pocket rag to wipe sweat or to cover up coughing or sneezing. If the chef was sloppy, then the pressure for cooks to wash their hands whenever they stepped out of line was not effcctive. It was the true culture of all Indians, Indonesians, and Filipinos on board the ship to carry with them when going to the toilet a little white bucket with water to wash their bottom instead of using toilet paper. It was fun to listen to these guys. Whenever using their hands, they would be making a splash splash sound. It is still indecent to continue such a practice while working and handling any food or beverage. Even if I didn't see or hear them, still their cabin carried an odor. That raw smell was permanent because their wash bucket was not sanitized or bleached, from what I experienced amongst the crew. I strongly believed that in the future all applicants should have taken a sanitation class before applying for the job, especially the dining room personnel, They were the main failure on board the ship when it came to public health. I saw many times both waiters and busboys passing the silver rock through the machine, packing it too tightly, Such a practice was wrong. When polishing silver with a wet service towel, if food stains were stuck to the utensils, such stains would be forced off then polished clean. I was never lucky enough to see during all my years working amongst these nationalities at any time the use of a handkerchief for coughing or sneezing.

When they caught a common cold, I carefully studied their condition to find the answer. Most countrymen loved to room with each other. Once vacation was due for any of these guys, I would request to take up residence in that cabin unless someone had requested it ahead of me. Smoking was one of these guys' habits. Their cabin always smelled smoky as did their bed linen and clothing. After dining room service was over, drinking and smoking became a top priority, and at bed time, without any pride, both feet would be washed in the face wash basin. That was their shower for the night. Some did not brush their teeth before bed, neither in the morning. As the morning arrived only to start a new and pressuring day, my roommate and I got up at the same time so we could get groomed and ready for work. Either one of us could use the mirror before the other. It was not a problem. We were both flexible with the timing. What I saw that morning was amazing. My cabin mate did not take a shower last night, neither did he take one this morning. In front of the mirror, he was using his ten fingers with water to comb his hair. He then used two fingers to clean his eyes. Sometimes he changed his shirt and would spray cologne around his neck and his clothing. The dirtiest part of these waiter uniforms were their shoes. They never stayed clean. In spite of the frequent complaints from passengers, the situation remained the same. It was so embarrassing. As a waiter, your passenger would be laughing and talking with you and at the same time he or she would be uncomfortable because of a bad-smelling odor both from your body and uniform. Passengers also complained about bad breath, especially when it came from alcohol, which is common amongst the men.

On many occasions, I was fortunate to catch dining room staff leaving the restroom without washing their hands. Several times, I caught waiters and busboys in the juice station drinking from the same glass intended to be served to the passenger. Personally, I condemn such practices that these mixed nationalities produced. Sometimes after lunch was over, the complete staff stayed behind to have their lunch. I shook my head after observing one of the waiters take a teaspoon from the table to eat a bowl of ice cream. Either he sent it back to the wash or just polished it and replaced it on table—anything was possible. It was a busboy's regular practice also to drink water from the drug. Touching food was a common assault that management tried hard to stop. It was a common practice for busboys to carry tea bags in their pockets. It was a kind of shortcut by not to present the tea box which contained a wide variety of regular tea and herbal teas. During the eighties, when I moved from utility to busboy, I carefully noticed that whenever a mixed-nationality waiter dropped any utensil on the carpet that same piece of silver would go back in the silver drawer. Millions of passengers and thousands of crew members both complained about the waiters' condition during the period from busboy to waiter. I heard passengers constantly asking for a slice of lemon to kill the taste of chlorine in the drinking water. Without any chlorine, the water would carry a different taste. Still, most things that happened on board were beyond the knowledge of the main office on shore side, until passenger comment cards reached them with such complaints. The water problem would not improve unless the tank was emptied and cleaned, especially the older ships. On some cruise lines, purified bottled water was sold to the passengers, and the crew bought their own bottled water from the stores on shore side. Too often passengers complained about the food being awful. From my experience, the problem could be cured with less pressure and an increase in salary.

Chapter-18

Charter cruises were predictable where hard work was concerned, also fixing by the dining room management, confusion, bad passenger behavior, and slim chance for an excellent mark. The word *group* or *charter* means the same to every crew member on board. There is no difference between them except for during a full charter cruise the daily program could be changed. Instead of sailing the regular run, the crew would get the opportunity to visit new islands. People on a charter cruise that came especially to eat would create a hard time for the chef and his men because there always were a few who were different and liked to eat up to three dishes per night. One passenger might notice that his fellow passenger in front of him had a different item that looked better, but sometimes one could be deceived by the presentation that a simple dish carried. Therefore, the dish became irresistible. Such temptation would cause the passenger to demand the same dish from the waiter. The waiter could not refuse to serve an extra dish. The head waiter would sign an extra ticket for the waiter to order the dish from the chef. Some passengers tried to eat more than the others. I overheard many times the statement, "Why pay the same fare and let you eat more than I do?" With this kind of mentality, the chef frequently ran out of certain items. The waiters kept running back and forth from the dining room to the kitchen for more food extras and exchanges. A majority of the waiters were already sweating for their day's pay.

Generally when the waiters learned that the group or charter was prepaid, it meant that the tip was sure to be worse. If the dining room personnel was informed by the management on board that the passengers could sit wherever they pleased, this also meant that the service standard would be dropped because such passengers never received a comment card. When people like these were not assigned to a table, only in the morning for breakfast, it caused a problem between the waiters because the work was not shared fairly. A waiter with a twenty station was sometimes fortunate that only four out of twenty turned up for breakfast. But unfortunately for him, ten more people entered the dining room and instead of sitting with their waiter they went and sat with the other four people because they were friends so this waiter ended up serving fourteen people while the other waiter took a walk.

On a charter cruise, it was like a crazy house. Everybody was rushing in and out of other cabins, trying not to miss any form of activity. For those who used powder, the bathroom definitely called for a deep cleaning. Also, those who ate lunch at the pool café would carry their leftovers to their cabins, which was more work for the cabin stewards. The fire patrol men also stayed on top of things because there were those who were under the influence of alcohol who would go around pushing the fire alarm button and squeezing out the fire extinguisher. Because of such behavior, when the cruise came to an end, most of us crew members were very happy indeed.

Chapter-19

There was such a thing as an emergency work break, which was different from the regular vacation. There were companies that required us to work three months from the date we signed on board the vessel before we could be entitled to a work break, but if there was a tragic accident that caused serious injury or death before the three-month period was fulfilled, the company would let us go home. Such an emergency was more effective, especially when it involved close family. Most crew members abused this opportunity by taking full advantage of it just to satisfy their needs and pleasure. Any member of their families, when asked to do so, would send a false emergency to the company that their mother was sick or dead. They would also send men on vacation and work break after a period of six months. Regardless, most company contracts were for one year. Within that period, if a crew member's performance was not up to standard, or if a crew member seemed tired, the company would send the individual on a work break, which could be from four to six weeks. There were other men who were already on their work break and vacation and were looking to return to the ship. It was like a wheel turning; there were always men standing by. A few crew members took emergency breaks often. Their mothers would die up to three times before the company caught up with them. When we were in our peak season, the ship was full to its capacity, and orders from shore side to the vessel informed us that no one would be getting work breaks after so many months. This was when the crew members came in with the emergency breaks dishonestly because it was insane to tell a man that he could not take an emergency break to see his sick wife; that was outrageous.

There was a system that was implemented by the management in the early eighties that I found very interesting and supportive. This system was organized only by the dining room personnel. Whichever one of us had a serious emergency, like a member of our family passed away, one person would go around and collect donations from everybody. Each man would give generously. I was that man who was collecting the money. I counted it and told the dining room manager the total I came up with and then delivered it in person to our fellow crew member who was departing to attend his mother's funeral. Some guys told lies just to get the money because it was time for them to go for vacation and they were dead broke. Most of these guys had served in the army back home and had a very tough life and lacked many things. They came west with the same doctrine of lying and stealing. How could one grandmother die more than once physically? I later learned that this was an organized crime game planned by these mixed nationalities. When it was time to collect to support these men from the east, and all Caribbean personnel supported this cause, the person who was receiving the donation would be observing very closely if all his fellow waiters and busboys were giving money to him. I could not come to myself up to this very moment, that the time would truly come for a member of the dining room staff to collect for my cause. It really happened; my mother passed away. The news broke because the telex came at sea. No one regarded the death of my mother except for one Caribbean waiter who was a Jamaican. He gave me twenty U.S. dollars. Not one European, Indonesian, Indian, or Filipino in my department asked me what was the cause of her death. I learned my lesson well.

Chapter-20

Each time a new recruit landed in the United States, from the moment customs and immigration was through with that person, he/she was on his/her own. It was a fact that not all companies picked up their new arrivals. Some companies would either send an agent or a bus, depending on how many men they knew were arriving that day. There were companies that were cheaper than others. If that was the case, one would have to take a taxi to his/her destination. The old-timers knew their way around like which number bus to travel on or the rail, anything that would drop them off within three to four blocks of the office; they would walk the rest. It was very economical if the hotel was within walking distance, up to one mile. Crew members would walk, especially if they were in a group. Sometimes they would put their money together and pay for a cab. On medical occasions, there were companies that transported crew members to and from. Whether you were in the hospital, on shore side, or in a hotel, when it was time to return to the ship, it was the company's responsibility to transport the crew. The kind of traveling crew members loved the most was long distance or from state to state or country to country, which required flying.

I flew from the States to Vancouver, British Columbia, once, and I got to sit beside an airplane pilot. I told him all I knew about ships, and he told me all he knew about airplanes. I watched the in-cabin movie. I slept and woke twice. I remember looking through the window, and the gentleman beside me asked me what I saw out there. I said to him, "I see nothing but swamps."

He laughed and then said to me, "It is not swamps. You are looking at lakes." Poor me, I was just an island boy; what did I know about lakes looking down from the skies? The kind of traveling we loved most was from coast to coast, two hundred miles and over. If the number of crew members was between twenty-five and thirty-five, the company would provide a large bus. This was a five-hour drive. We would stop twice at the rest places to use the toilet and once for lunch, but in my group we provided and carried with us an open bar, simply rum and Coke with ice, and music, and we would stay in the back seat and party. Other crew members would join in too. Some guys rented a car to suit their purpose. Only on occasion I would rent a car and spend two hours in town before we started our journey. If the bus driver was cool, we would ask him to stop at the mall so we could pick up a few items. Some crew members stopped at the bank to make a withdrawal. There were times when the company would fly us to a small island to wait upon the arrival of the ship.

Only a few immigration officers I found to be intelligent, upright, and very friendly. I remember my first entrance through the airport. The lines were super long. People from all walks of life filled this big checking area. I had never seen so many immigration officers in my life. There were at least thirty immigrants in front of me. Because it was my first time, I started to look all over the room. I did not know their laws or procedures, but I noticed one line on my right said, "United States citizens and residents only," and to my left was "Visitors only." I said to myself, "This looks like separating the sheep from the goats." When I looked around me again, I noticed I had to look really hard to recognize the few West Indians that were present. The other people looked Spanish, European, and Oriental. The line moved fairly well. It also depended on the paperwork to be processed and the number of people traveling together. Everything seemed to be in the right mood until I reached the inspecting officer. "Good morning," I said and handed him all my documents including my return ticket valued for one year according to my contract and my passport with my seaman visa, also valued for one year. My passport and visa were tested to ensure they were not bogus. His computer should have linked up with the company computer to confirm my arrival. A dated company letter was addressed directly to the immigration authorities. This was to certify that I was employed by this company as a buffet runner, and it went on to state that I was presently in transit to join such ship registered in such country sailing out of such port on such day, and any assistance given to the above would be greatly appreciated. The personnel manager signed the letter after thanking the authorities for their cooperation. The letter included the company's phone number and full address, telex, and fax. Also available was my contract with my position and monthly salary and another letter that directed me to the above hotel with full address and phone number of where I would be staying at the company's expense. My medical papers and x-ray charts proved that I entered the country in shipshape condition. With all this paperwork, the officer still put me in a small room where I waited for over an hour before they gave me back all my documents and told me I could go just like that. In the same room with me were three other Caribbean visitors, and all the other people I mentioned above went through without a second check. I felt so embarrassed when the officer called another officer to escort me to the inspecting room. At that first moment, all the other visitors were looking at me as if my entry was illegal.

During my second vacation, when I returned back to the States, I still had in mind that I might end up back in the same room again, but this time it was completely different. This officer was highly intelligent and went through the paperwork and saw that everything was up to date and legal. This was where I started to have two opinions about the mixed nationalities. Most of the immigration officers were

Cubans, and there were a few Caucasians who believed in giving distant people with good morals problems.

After I completed my second full year, I went on vacation again and returned to the States for the third time. As the plane came to a complete stop, everyone started to move from their seats. As I entered the door to step outside, there were two men standing there. They must have been narcotics officers. They stopped only the people they believed were from the Caribbean and searched their things. One of the men was rude to me. After being asked what I was doing here, I answered, "To work." He started to push a thin piece of wire through my little basket that I was carrying with two cakes that my mother-in-law had baked for me, because the hotel food was a little hard on my stomach. Whenever I skipped meals, I would munch on my cakes. This nincompoop was looking for drugs. As soon as he was finished, I entered the immigration line for inspection. After that I was sent to the small room again for the second time. One of the immigration officers told me that if the agent from the company refused to pick me up, they would arrange a flight the following day for me to return to my country. It was hours before the agent arrived.

But I would like to express my true feelings that I am happy to know and to say that none of us as Caribbean people are terrorists or heads of any organized crime against humanity or anti-American. We are not such people as the Unibomber or give any kind of bomb threat. We are not the kind of people who would try to bomb the World Trade Center and target airplanes or bomb our own city homes, women, and children. We have human dignity within.

Chapter-21

In the early eighties when applying for a job on board any ship that I worked on, safety training was not required, but a full health examination was. No cruise line could afford to send a new crew member on board their vessel with any kind of virus. It really bothered me which came first,—was it health, money, or safety? What should I say? Whether it was intentional or not, passengers did cruise with various kinds of illnesses. As passengers continued to board with their viruses such as pink eye and chicken pox, the ones serving them were us the healthy ones. A virus such as a cold could take a long time to get rid of because of the many compartments of steel in the ceilings and walls. They all started out with a lot of sneezing and coughing, and in no time, all the crew members were visiting the doctor in the infirmary. If a crew member was not seriously ill, the ship's doctor would recommend aspirin for his flu. As for the officers who showed up, the doctors would give them some stronger medicine. In any event, when walking behind the passengers or crew members, if anyone should sneeze or cough, I would immediately hold my breath until I cleared that zone. While serving a passenger with a bad flu, I noticed that both my nostrils were running. On returning to my cabin at any rest period, I made sure to take two cold tablets before bed. I never gave any virus time to develop maximum strength.

The health-care plan was not satisfactory to me. First, it started with the contract that we signed explaining the insurance coverage for all employees' injuries and illnesses and the medical facilities. The main medical office on shore side with the insurance agreement was responsible for our medical treatment, whether we were admitted to the nearest hospital or had an appointment to see the dentist or to see a specialist. The contract also stated that while a crew member was signed off the vessel, whether it was for a work break or vacation, there was no insurance coverage. The fulfillment of a contract was one year. Taking a work break was something we were entitled to after the first three months, depending on how tired one felt, up to six or nine months before vacation was due. We could take a work break to go home to rest for a short period of time then return to finish our contract. There were other cruise lines that gave vacations per six-month periods. A few crew members who wanted fast treatment would break the company policy by seeking an outside doctor first. Some crew members definitely did not believe in the ship's doctors for many reasons.

One day, I found myself feeling very sick but not weak. I continued to work until the next day. I continued to feel worse. The company policy was that the head of the department would give us a form to fill out on which we would state the problem being experienced then sign at the bottom. Some doctors would see a crew member without the paper but with a protest. The form we filled out gave us full authorization for medical treatment from the ship's doctor. That day at the doctor's office, after he examined me, I received some medication and was told to return if further problems developed, After taking all my medication, I still visited the doctor with the same problem. I now felt like a laboratory rat after receiving more tablets with my second authorization form. The only good thing about my second visit was that the doctor gave me two days off. My illness did not improve, so the doctor made me an appointment to see a specialist in St. Thomas Virgin Island. The ship agent received my document that stated that I should see a specialist. Instead, the agent took me to see an MD. I bet my life that this agent charged the cruise line a fee for a specialist, or maybe he just disregarded the company rules. This MD to me sounded like he did not know anything about my problem. I went back to work after gaining a little strength that day. During the following cruise, I decided that upon arrival in Puerto Rico I would do myself a favor by breaking the company policy by visiting an outside doctor. I asked my supervisor for the time off. The thing I loved about him was that he understood my position. Taxi drivers in Puerto Rico were very nice people. I asked one driver to please take me to a very good doctor. For the first time in my life, I sat before a Spanish doctor. He asked me what was wrong. I explained. This doctor made it sound so simple when he told me it was gastroenteritis. Returning to the ship that afternoon, I handed over the bill to the management on board. It was in vain to do so, but still I tried.

Chapter-22

In the dining room, without the knowledge of the main office on shore side, the treatment of the Caribbean men and other nationalities was not on the same level. I agreed that just a few dining room managers were not partial. On occasion, waiters and busboys would withdraw from their duties. The ship's doctor's commands depended on the type of illness. It was the dining room management's duty to use the two nearest waiters to fill the gap of the other waiter that the doctor relieved from duty, either Caribbean or another nationality. What I noticed with some ignorant, unintelligent, uncivilized, hurry-come-up dining room management was that once a Caribbean waiter was sick and another man of a different nationality was next to him, they would always look to see if there was a Caribbean waiter also close by. If so, the head waiter would certainly ask the island boy to serve the table and bypass the other nationalities. A full ship also created a problem for waiters and busboys when feeling ill and how they would go about it. A dining room staff person may have his girlfriend cruising on a particular voyage without the knowledge of anyone, which was much safer for his job. He was either planning to tell the dining room manager during the five-fifteen meeting or after the meeting was finished that he was feeling sick and unable to perform his duty this cruise. This kind of approach could really get any maitre d' mad after spending half of the day making the stations for over a hundred men. With a full ship, a majority of the stations were so large that some men could hardly handle it, and suddenly someone showed up sick. It was much better if a waiter or busboy showed up much earlier in the day, maybe the maitre d' could have done something for him. Suppose he was truly sick; would the maitre d's action have been the same? Yes, he would still have gotten mad. If one's condition was not very low, the maitre d' would psychologically persuade the waiter with encouraging words like, "see if you can work for me tonight" and "come see me in the morning; I will give you a paper to see the doctor." When the ship was empty, no one cared if ten men were sick at one time because we always had a lot of standbys who were not working. Sickness was a reproach to any man. While sick, some of us continued to work, for this reason. I did not respect some maitre d's.

On another occasion, I received a referral from the ship's doctor to see a shore-side doctor due to my condition. One head waiter brought over the envelope to my station and handed it to me. He asked me to open it. He needed to check the appointment time. It was 9:30 AM the next morning. As stated, the pickup service was at 7:45 AM. The head waiter told me he would split my station, which is the right system. Later that same evening, the assistant maitre d' asked what time my appointment was. I told him I had a nine-thirty appointment to see the doctor and my pickup service was at seven forty-five. The maitre d' told me that I could still work until 9 AM in the morning. Knowing that he was breaking the system, I immediately disagreed with him. As he departed from my presence, I noticed that he and the other head waiter that brought over the envelope were talking. Shortly, the head waiter returned to me and insisted that I work until 9 AM. With many years of experience in this system, I told him that if I was another nationality, I personally would not be experiencing this madness. Without another word, he walked away. Neither of those two living dead could have matched me with words because they knew the truth and it hurt. The maitre d' called me and asked me what the story was about other nationalities. I told him, "Please don't raise your voice at me. I am not a child. If anyone wants me to show them respect, they must also show respect to me. I have been sick over a month now, and my pickup service is at 7:45 AM, and the head waiter is still insisting that I work."

The maitre d' pointed out to me another waiter and said, "His appointment is also at nine thirty, and he is also working until nine. Why can't you?" The maitre d' said, "You can go, you can." I did not like the look of his eyes. Neither did I trust his words. It was because of how he said it. Those words did not sound right to me. Moreover, he was not pleased with me.

On embarkation morning, the assistant maitre d' told me I could go because I was much smarter than the rest of the guys. During the main seating of breakfast, I paid the infirmary a visit to investigate what was true from false. Fortunately for me, the company lawyer was there waiting for some kind of information pertaining to some kind of lawsuit. In front of the lawyer, the nurse asked me what the problem was. I showed my form and asked her, "Is this the time stated I should go by?"

She said yes. I told her the dining room management was forcing me to work. The lawyer then got involved in the conversation and told me that I had to obey the doctor's order, and the time he set on the form was what I should go by.

"Thank you, sir," I said to him and left. Only on occasion when a crew member was in a serious condition would the ship authorities turn around to the nearest island to surrender the sick, after a long decision. On two occasions, I could say that two crew members were dead after being surrendered.

Chapter-23

People from all over the world found it difficult to obtain a United States visa either to enter or reenter, especially deportees or criminals who would seek the most fortunate way possible. Sea craft were their main objective, and the cost they paid per head in the mid-eighties, according to the rumor, 5,000 us;to say how many stowaways per week might make it,

I cannot say, and to say how many stowaways is unfortunate on their attempt would be misleading. At any seaport that carried five or more ships, whether they were cargo ships or cruise ships, the port and the waterfront became very busy, and that was the right timing for the stowaway to get on board. Ships that stayed overnight were also easy for anyone to get on board. This was big business, depending on how many stowaways a crew could handle. Most crew members preferred to do stowaways over drugs. Because police dogs could not sniff out stowaways, why would anyone care to bother with illegal drugs?

I learned my way in the pirate world and the whole procedure in setting up an operation in the Bahamas, the closest islands to the States. Most people who came to this little island would state that the nature of their visit would be either vacation or business with the intention to run off. When their stay was up, they would disregard all immigration rules and regulations and immediately become illegal immigrants. The fortunate ones who had friends and family would hide out for a while. Unfortunately, there were those who did not have such privileges after their hotel money ran out. Now they became desperate. Even if their spending money was done under heaven, their stowaway money would not be touched. It was much better for them to beg than to use their stowaway money. Also, they never came down to the dock to make any form of negotiation. The clever ones knew that the fastest way to get caught by immigration was in the early morning when the immigration officers stormed the buses searching for proper identification. At night, they also would storm the nightclub that the crew members hung out in. At the night club, all bargaining took place while the music played. The stowaways were a reproach to any crew member. If any crew member needed the money because of a low-salary income, the chance was likely to be taken. Both crew member and stowaway would carefully organize and come to a mutual understanding. A stowaway must remember everything that a crew member informed him about the internal structure of the ship. Back in the nightclub, special precaution had to be taken because in every illegal system, there would always be an undercover cop. To bring a stowaway on board. He needed a crew pass for himself to go through, and the crew had to provide him with one. If the quartermaster could be bribed, the whole operation was ten times easier. The quartermaster's job was to stop and inspect all unauthorized persons at the gangway who tried to make such an attempt, but if he was in on the operation, up to twenty stowaways on all the vessels could be done each week. A crew member with an extra pass was very important for this kind of business. In this kind of case, most crew members always reported to the chief crew steward or head of department that their shore pass was lost just to obtain a second pass. Very few quartermasters knew all the faces of the crew and were very hard to deceive. Whenever there was a new face, whether it be crew member or stowaway, the quartermaster would stop them and closely examine their crew pass. But once the quartermaster saw other crew members walking and talking with each other, chances were that he would not stop the new face but watch him to see if he would change his pass. The fact was that all stowaways were briefed, ready, and aware that the quartermaster would watch their movements. All the crew members that were involved would crowd around the stowaway to prevent the quartermaster from a close inspection. If the new face was lucky to pass the gangway, he had to remember to make the right turns because this would be the turn of his future.

Plan A was to bring him on board; plan B was to keep him unknown until the arrival in the States. On board a person may look new, but we the crew never put much thought into it because fresh groups of crew members signed on actually every cruise, even old-timers. Sometimes a week would pass before we ran into each other. In order for a stowaway to make it to the States, he could not leave the cabin, not even for a short walk. He could not have his meals in the crew mess. Whoever he was paying had to bring his food to the room. He could not go to the toilet without being escorted if it was an outdoor toilet. He was not allowed to play music in the cabin when he was alone. It was a must that he exited the cabin once for the captain's inspection. When a new face was suspected, the crew would hide him in the locker, especially if someone knocked on the door. Any crew member who was involved in this kind of operation knew of the risks and the consequences behind it. They knew from the start that their job was on the line and they could possibly go to jail.

The ships that stayed overnight in these ports were great for this kind of business. At night, stowaways would climb up by the ropes, then they would change into dry clothing immediately. There were times when the quartermaster suspected or luckily caught one and called the bridge to report the matter directly to the safety officer. The safety officer would call the security officer and tell him to get more men and meet him on the bridge, where the plan was to search the ship floor by floor, cabin by cabin. If the crew members were sleeping, they would be awakened and be questioned. Sometimes it was a false alarm. If this person was caught, the captain and other officers would interrogate him. If a new face wanted another chance because of this failure, it was best for him not to mention any names. Getting off the ship was much easier for stowaways. They just walked off over and over. Sometimes the quartermaster noticed that I walked through without changing my pass and asked me to do so; if a crew member only needed to make a call on the dock and returned, the quartermaster normally told us to go ahead. the immigration and all officer on board are not highly intelligent to stop this illegal activity. When a new face got busted, he was detained until we arrived in the States, where arrangements were made for his deportation. Some new faces escaped when we just about entered the channel. They did not care which side of the ship it was because jumping was the only alternative to attain freedom. Some jumped to life, while others jumped to their death.

Chapter-24

In Ilaugra Venezuela, arriving into port that morning, as far as my eyes could behold, the whole view of the hillside to the level of the town, the standard of living spoke for itself. Most of the stores there used a person who spoke proper English to be the supervisor because this was a Spanish-speaking country. Shopping in this little town was very much affordable against the dollar. Crew members uselessly tried to get lucky with the girls outside; there was no chance of corresponding. It was a very poor chance to find a girl. The crew would have to take a bus or a taxi of a far faster speed to Caracas. At that time long ago, girls were very cheap—only seven U.S. dollars and the older women five dollars. Soldiers were always on the street with their guns. I did not see any police on duty. The cruise director always told the passengers that shorts were not allowed when getting off the ship and neither was it good for anyone to run or go jogging. Crime was low in this part of the country.

When we finally docked in Grenada, a representative from the tourist board would board the vessel to speak to the passengers through the P.A. system and explain every detail about their country just to promote a good day's shopping. I did not believe such information was done properly or with regard to this country by whoever was in charge of this country. There were a lot of mountains in Grenada, and the people there were friendly to visitors. To see the island better and cheaper, it was best to take a local bus and pay for a round trip so you would see more for your money; the standard of living also spoke for itself. The crime rate was not bad. The bishop movement did not discourage me to look on the beauty and the friendliness of the people. This was a little great place for tourists. Their airport run way was the best of the Caribbean islands.

Barbados was one of my favorite ports. I could go just about anywhere without looking over my shoulder. The people there were friendly to visitors. Tourism was one of their main resources, along with sugarcane. The port authorities provided a bus service for us to the main terminal exit free of charge. This was very convenient to the crew members and passengers. The girls in Barbados were very nice along the main street downtown. We called it Broad Road. A lot of young men were strung out in a long line with their backs against the wall trying to seduce the young ladies as they passed by. I must not forget to mention the dock in Barbados. It was the best dock in the Caribbean. The restaurant and food there was great. Also there was only one place in Barbados that attracted the crew members most, which was Nelson Street. All the girls and day clubs could be found there. Only by chance would you find a native girl in one of these girl shops.

The island of Martinique was a beautiful place to visit. The mountain side is green and attractive; the soil is moist and rich; and the rain forest gave you a sense of where nature belonged. The main town in Martinique was very historical and informative when explained by the natives. This was the first island in the Caribbean to install a nuclear power plant to supply the island with electricity. What I noticed was that there were different nationalities living there as well. This little French island taxi driver was courteous and informative during the tours. Shopping in Martinique was very affordable to us the crew. Sailing alongside the west coast of Martinique was always a pleasure for us. We would position ourselves at the back of the ship and admire the dolphins. Once in a while, we ran into a few whales. Most of the natives that we met were super nice to the bone. I appreciated this island because of the low crime rate. The main tourist attraction in Martinique was their volcano, which could be seen from a far distance off shore whenever approaching the port. There was also an observation lab that the tour guide showed us across the next mountain. The lab was to monitor the volcano daily.

The island of wood and water, and out of many one people, with the word no problem was originate in Jamaica not to mention about irie and the word hey mon. The natives here were warm, and it was a great place to visit. Friendly taxi drivers were always standing by to take visitors wherever they wanted to go. The north coast's most attractive areas were Port Antonio, Ocho Rios, Montego Bay, and Negril Beach. Negril was famous for its seven miles of white sand beach. Still developing, Montego Bay was the best tourist resort; things would be much better for tourists if the governor coach went back into operation. Still, there was horseback riding across the mountain, plantation tours, rain forests, the Rose Hall Great House, the great river rafting, the straw market, and excellent beaches to fill the gap of the missing tourist train. I recommended that visitors take a local bus that would take them to different sections of the island; it was far cheaper and they ended up seeing more for their money. Ocho Rios was famous with the Dunns River falls; the beauty about the falls was that it could be climbed all the way to the top. Port Antonio, the east section of the island, carried more mountains and larger rain forests. Rafting was one of their main attractions. Also the overall crime rate was very low compared to other places with bomb threats and group movements.

Puerto Rico was the crew's favorite place, and I recommended it highly. I was surprised to see the big change on the main street since I have arrived there lately;

in the early eighties, there were a lot of bars and nightclubs that were situated on the front right across from where the ship docked. One night just before we set sail, there was a big fire on the main street that destroyed a couple of buildings. Still, this place was the crew's best shopping area, and it was quite affordable. The night life was great, and the casino kept you occupied. The forts of the old San Juan were very historical. Puerto Rico was also famous for its rum. The crime rate was the least concern.

The Bahamas could provide visitors with various kinds of attractions, and it all depended on which one of the islands one stayed. If one was looking for peace and quiet, Nassau would have to be avoided. Before I make any comment about this island, I must first say that I actually lived there. I- spent more of my time there than on any other island. Only a few ships stay overnight. Most of us crew members spend the whole night in nightclubs and casinos. It is much safer to take a taxi than to walk. The drug men and gunmen come out at nights. To be on the safe side, we always stayed on the front page during the night, and that depends on which section. The crew members that received the worst treatment from the natives were men from Jamaica. The Bahamas is not in the Caribbean. That is why they are totally different from us. Because of their close relation to the States, they are more Americanized. Once we got off the ship and turned left up the street, we could be in danger. Most natives came out at night for one reason only: to make trouble and if possible to hurt a crew member and brag about it. In their possession, they carried long knives, guns, and baseball bats. I remember one night while we were outside having the time of our lives, one crew member was almost beaten to death with a baseball bat. He ended up in the hospital with a broken jaw, and it hurt me to know that this crew member did not receive any help from the government from this island nor the company he worked for to catch any of these culprits even though these men could be seen on the street every night. All the nightclubs used a chuckaround because the natives loved to fight with the crew and didn't care how much we were right. They called us aliens, and that was what made us double wrong. All the day clubs and nightclubs on this particular street that played reggae music for the crew's listening pleasure were automatically closed down by the authorities because of the ignorant behavior of the natives. There were only two safe places on the island to which every cruise line would send their passengers out at night to enjoy themselves: the Paradise Island and Crystal Palace shows and casinos. If any passenger ended up elsewhere, he or she was independently doing so. The crime rate was high, and Foxhill was always full. I was on the island up to the time of March '96, when the hanging of one inmate took place by law. The main street was the front page, and that was the safest place in the downtown area because it carried maximum police security. It was a nice place to visit, but I recommended staying on the waterfront at night.

Chapter-25

The international phrase that was used by millions around the world was that "health comes first," and anything else came after. For anyone who took a course to become a public health officer, it was good. Nothing was wrong with that, but I still saw it on the theory side. I truly observed when public health inspectors came on board to conduct a full inspection, which was once every three months. Even if these inspections were conducted quarterly, that was not good enough. I believed that every four to six weeks, all vessels should get one visit or the public health officers should take the cruise to fully conduct a proper inspection under the courtesy of minimum expense like travel agents and immigration did. I had a good reason for saying these things. A month before the inspection showed up, the management on board would push the crew very hard to maintain a high standard of cleanliness. When public health officers were behind schedule, it was we the crew that ended up paying the price of an overextended pressure. Most times, the head of all departments was informed from shore side that the public health officers would be waiting for us in the morning. When the health officers were good in disguising themselves, the surprise would hit us very hard. But the best way to avoid public health pressure was to dock just a little later than usual. By doing so, the most delicate areas like the kitchen would be finished serving breakfast. Passengers and crew had been through this experience over and over. When public health officers were on board, the service became really slow. Management couldn't care less if the passengers complained and asked many questions including "what took our breakfast so long?" Our main concern during a public health inspection was to pass the test. Every worker, both on shore side and on board the vessel, certainly was nervous. Once we passed the public health test, the management on board would leave us alone until the next inspection drew near again. The only inspection we the crew had to worry about now was the captain's inspection plus inspections by every head of department on the last night once per week. If the ship failed, it would be a big problem and may the good Lord above help us because the pressure would now applied twice as much until the public health officers returned to conduct a re-inspection, and we had better pass with high marks this time. Because of the bad condition some ships were in, such vessels would purposely avoid all United States ports. A United States public health inspection was tougher than all the rest, and if I were to take a cruise in the future, I personally would choose a line that used a United States port as their main terminal.

As a crew member, I took note carefully on how these inspections were conducted. As the health inspection officers arrived, the first place they would head for was the food preparation areas like the kitchen, the dining room, the pool café, etc. Once they were in the kitchen, the inspectors would stand in different areas. One would be watching how the cook served and how the waiter received. One would be checking the hot and cold temperatures and a few items to see if they were sanitized and clean. In the kitchen, the waiters normally liked to use their fingers to arrange items more properly so that the presentation of the dish would look more presentable. On this particular day, everybody had to wear gloves. No touching with bare hands was allowed. If the cooks did not arrange the food properly, the waiter did not dare to reorganize it but to present it as it was to the passengers. In the dishwashing area, one inspector would be watching the busboys, mainly because they were the ones who carried out all the dirty dishes to be washed. There were two doors between the dining room and the kitchen: an entrance and an exit. The door that led from the dining room to the kitchen was where all the dirty things went through. Sometimes waiters with food would take a shortcut through that door, depending on where their station was located, and that could cause cross-contamination. As long as the public health officers were standing there, every dining room worker would have to use the right door to the kitchen and from the kitchen to the dining room. The line in the dishwashing area during a public health inspection automatically became very long. Normally on the last morning, breakfast was rushed and done by eight thirty. For some cruise lines, breakfast was over by nine thirty. If breakfast service on a normal basis passed the due time that we were used to, that meant something was very wrong. Normally the waiters' and busboys' behavior in the kitchen was like little kids playing in the classroom, but as their teacher entered the room, they became silent. That was what happened on the last morning when the public health inspectors were present. Their behavior and silence was supposed to impress the officers. After the first seating was over, it was time for the second seating. Passengers were going to experience the long wait before the dining room was open for breakfast. The dishwashers in the dishwashing area were certainly moving slow because they couldn't afford to make any mistakes, and some of the waiters and busboys who hated to wash their hands after taking out dirty dishes would certainly do so in front of a health inspector. In the dining room, the inspectors would stand and look around. If any cold item was left standing on top of the side stand, the person who left it was certainly foolish. The dining room staff would never do that. Some of them would take the chance and hide cold items under the bottom shelf of the side stand. The inspectors never looked inside the side stands. Most waiters kept their room keys and cigarettes and personal belongings in the top drawers, which were used to keep utensils. There were a lot of things the public health inspectors did not know, neither did they examine what they needed to. some practical lesson and observation on board, like for one full week while cruising, they can learn the system well.

Chapter-26

A thief comes in many style and forms, and there were many different types of thieves on board, starting with the passengers. Because I was a person who lived with expectations, it was very hard for me to be deceived by anyone. I knew there were normal people all over the world, but to be on the safe side, I had no choice but to put everybody in the same basket. Men were not perfect, and for that reason we as men became failures. Look at this man; he booked the cruise for one, maybe two if he needed the company. No one on board knew anything about him, and what was his achievement or the nature of his visit? It was to cause problems for the cruise line or to get rich quick. The first thing he was going to do was to pick a target, maybe an old rich couple who had no other interest in the cruise than to sit down and play cards in the cards room all day, or maybe he targeted a sun worshiper, or just sat in the library to study how much time other passengers spent reading. There were gamblers who spent most of their time in the casino. Whatever it was that kept any passenger up on deck was to his advantage. The two most entertaining decks during the day were the casino deck and the pool deck. A thief carefully studied his target for two days out of seven. Why two? He loved to move fast. The faster the thief moved, the more passengers he got to shake down. He would sit down, have a drink in his dark shades, and observe. As soon as his target decided to return to their cabin, the thief would carefully follow them to know the location of their room and their number. These people's next move from their cabin would be the last. Once the thief recognized these people back up on deck, it was time for him to go down. For a professional lock-picker, these kinds of doors were like taking candy from a baby. A wise passenger always opened a safety deposit box at the front desk, where his cash and valuables could be kept. On the other hand, when passengers realized how friendly their cabin stewards were, they were convinced to leave their valuables out. Certainly both the cabin steward and the company would bear a very bad name if a passenger ended up suing the cruise line, and most likely, the cabin steward would lose his job when a bad record was attached to his file. The best day for a thief was port day. Ninety-five percent of the passengers and crew would leave for shore, leaving behind a completely empty ship and giving enough room for a thief. He also picked credit cards that the cruise line issued to the passengers. Normally passengers would report the missing credit card to the front desk.

Another thing I learned was that all management on board carried a master key, and generally all over the world it has been evidently proven both locally and internationally that thieves, deceivers, and wicked men are in high places. There is none that is righteous—no, not one. Management had all the privileges to open any door they wanted to or when they needed to, whether it was opening or locking for either passengers or crew members who had lost or locked their key behind them. Over and over, a crew member would be on duty and after finishing working would return to his cabin only to find out that his cabin had been broken in to. When it was not valuables, it was his whole life's savings gone with the wind. Nobody knew who had taken it because there were no eye witnesses. Also, there was no compensation for their loss. Everyone on board was told to either open a safety deposit box on board or bank their savings on shore side, which was much safer. Management who were trafficking drugs made it look too easy. They hardly ever got searched—or I should say never. The only time they did get searched by the narcotics force was when they had been informed on.

The dining room management were other big crooks. They had multiple ideas of how to steal and get rich. Of those that I experienced, their plan was to sell days off. In my earlier days, a day off cost seventy U.S. dollars. The phrase *day off* does not mean a complete day; it is a lunch off only. There were three open seating lunches within a cruise, depending on whether it was a seven-day cruise or less. Both waiters and busboys were due for days off by rotation. When the dining room manager sold someone an extra day off, what really happened was the pressure definitely reached the other guys who did not pay. So, instead of getting two port days off, these poor guys got only one day off for the cruise. The waiters and busboys who bought the day off, the dining room manager made sure at all times that these special guys received a larger station than the others where they could make better money. The dining room manager never collected this mafia money in person; he would allow the assistant maitre d' to collect from us in order to protect himself. In this operation, only the old-timers got this kind of opportunity. The new boys could not be trusted yet. The word *station* meant how many tables a waiter and a busboy served. There were tables of ten, eight, six, four, and two. And by right, the rating that the waiters made from the passengers should have determined the station they received. On the other hand, a waiter's station could be determined in many ways, and the two persons that were responsible for making these decisions were the dining room manager and his assistant, and this was how it was done. The dining room manager had his favorite guys that he liked, and in that sense, even if the waiter came in with a low rating, this same waiter would remain at the same station from which he should have been moved. By right, if this waiter was consistent in making the rating and failed once or twice, this waiter would remain in the same station. If during the next cruise, this same waiter's rating was still low, then he would be moved to a smaller station. The ones that the dining room manager did not like would pay a price of not making enough money. The maitre d' could dislike one for many reasons. You could either talk too much or maybe you liked to fight with your fellow crew members. For this reason, the maitre d' would look upon you as a troublemaker. Maybe the waiter was a playboy with the underage passenger ladies or maybe he reported to work late too often. Sometimes if you were smarter than the maitre d' when holding discussions, he would claim that you were arguing with him, and that also determined the size of your station. A station also could be decided by payment. Most crooked maitre d's would sell the waiter their station just like what was done with the days off. The maitre d' sold beer and soft drinks to us after every lunch and dinner. The guys who bought the most beer from his bar ended up getting a large station. Now, sometimes both the maitre d' and the assistant would disagree over who received the stations. If the assistant disliked anyone, he would pump the maitre d' to sign whoever the busboy or waiter was to a smaller station. If either of these two men really did not like you, you had to try your best not to get any negative complaints from the passengers. It was even worse if the complaint came from an open seating. This would give the maitre d' and his assistant more strength and reason to dislike you and then penalize you.

We also had a system that we called prepaid, which simply meant that the passenger already paid everything in advance, which covered food, boarding, and tips. Most of us as waiters and busboys loved when it was a prepaid cruise. I was not blind to the fact that we could be cheated. There were dining room management that were big-time crooks. There were times when sixteen people were traveling together, which was a complete station for most waiters, with two tables of eight. The dining room manager would carefully split the group of sixteen between two waiters like a block away. It was hard for us to recognize that we were serving a group. It took one with good intelligence and foresight to see that these people were prepaid. At the end of the cruise, we the waiters would notice that the passengers would get up from around the table and leave without tipping. If we were stupid, we would just say to ourselves that these people were very cheap and that would be wrong. Sometimes we believed that these passengers were real lowlifes, plus it was wrong for us to ask them for our tip. We normally hoped and prayed that the following cruise things would be better. The prepaid money that rightfully belonged to us would now be shared between the dining room management because they lacked integrity. When a big group chartered the cruise, everything was free except the bar on some lines. The group didn't have to buy sodas. Our money for the charter cruise was handed over to the dining room manager the following cruise to pay all personnel. Nobody had any knowledge that the money was already handed over to the maitre d'. The maitre d' used the cruise to figure out how much money he could dishonestly take for himself. During the second cruise, everybody started to ask each other one question: When is the prepaid money going to be paid to us? So, even if the maitre d' was slow and needed some more time to check out how much he could make off the waiters and busboys, he now had to cut his study short because everyone was on the hyper side. In the middle of the cruise, the maitre d' would keep a very short meeting just to inform us that he would be paying the money today. The first thing he would tell us was, "Sorry, boys. This group paid one dollar short." None of us was surprised. Everybody knew the business with the prepaid money. There was this certain dining room manager who, whenever he cheated us out of our prepaid money, would start to explain the money to us in points. Point this and point that was taken from point so and so equal to point this. That was like law he was laying down, but as I said before, everybody knew the business.

On the last night of the cruise, both waiters and busboys had to pay out of their tips, which the ship terminology for this collection was *tax*. All the waiters would pay more than the busboys for more than one reason. The first reason was that after the midnight buffet was finished every night, the buffet men who worked in the cold food preparation would set up the tables through the whole dining room for us waiters. In the morning, when we waiters returned for breakfast, all we had to do was recheck the tables to make sure the utensils, china wares, and tablecloths were clean. From our tips, money was drawn to pay these men. The second reason was waiters had to pay less than a dollar for each passenger's head that was assigned to his table for the whole cruise. This money went into the hands of the dining room manager. The guys that worked in the dishwashing area must also receive some of our money, but how much did they receive? There was another guy who worked in the main office on shore side; he was called the corporate manager for the dining room. He was in charge of all the dining room managers working with this company. He was one guy that could get rich very quickly. There was no secret on board the ship, because a waiter without any class or even the ability to speak proper English was fit and ready to be a head waiter, and a waiter that wanted to be a head waiter it will cause them from six thousand dollars up to nine thousand. No wonder there were so many bad managers on board the vessel. In the good old days, I applied for this job and received my contract in less than a month; it was not so now. Any position away from the dining room was going to cost from six hundred dollars up. A dining room was going to cost a lot more, and who were these guys that were selling the job? There were agents that were doing so. Such agents could work independently, or if not, he would work alongside an undercover manager without the knowledge of the bigger boss. These guys made a lot of money because most of the men I talked with told me that they knew guys that got ripped off. Raffling appliance and other items I knew of, not even the dump would receive them, I also consider that a ripped off. I have seen the dining room management help the shore side management to raffle all different kinds of items, and in their own unique ways, everybody was told to buy a ticket or they would make sure to give the non-purchasers a small station. The management said this in a joking manner, still nobody trusted that kind of joke. To prevent any obstacle in our lives we all purchased a ticket.

The next thief on board was the guy who took drugs. The cabins he targeted mostly were the waiters', busboys', cabin stewards', and passengers'. These four cabins were targeted, especially the dining room staff. They got the most hits. This crew member who got hooked on drugs knows the working hours and would time all his targeted cabins to make his move. To get hold of a master key was not a problem. It was a must that he should break into these cabins to steal money to supply his drug addict needs. Drugs also made these victims sell everything they possessed that carried value.

Gambling was a very bad and insensitive habit for any crew member. I learned many things from other people's mistakes, and gambling was one of the prime ones. Crew members from the Philippines, India, and Europe loved to gamble. They would go to the casino every cruise, and once this casino got into their system, it was hard for them to get rid of it. Every country that provided casinos for tourists also welcomed crew members. For anyone to take up casino full-time, all they needed was a little encouragement from an old

gambler. All seaman knew that there was an advance coupon for crew members only. At the casino entrance, all crew members had to do was approach the cashiers and show them our crew pass and sign for our coupon, which was thirty dollars. After that, we would walk all over the casino to find an empty table and hand the coupon to a second cashier. This cashier would in turn give us some chips to the value of the coupon in exchange. If the amount was not enough for us, we normally reached for our wallet to add to what we received for free. Whichever game we wanted to play was up to us. In all my years as a seaman, I never saw a crew member leave as a big winner. The fact was that everyone on board worked very hard. This was not an easy life for us unless someone wanted to lie about it. Seventy hours per week was the least every man worked according to the contract we signed. The salary was not that great, and payday was every two weeks. It was a shame to see some of the men take their paycheck to the casino with the intention of gambling half and ending up losing their complete pay with nothing left but an empty wallet and a taxi fare to take them back to the ship. Casino gambling was not for the crew members who came from a poor family background or were working hard just to make something good out of life. I felt sorry for some because they became addicted. Within one cruise, we ran into two casinos. In the first casino, you would find a lot of crew members becoming broke. Before reaching the second casino, these crew members started to bother their fellow crew members for a loan until the next payday. For us, payday always took a long time to come around. When it was payday, these crew members would pay out everything and stay broke until the next payday came. Not all of these gamblers were honest. These crew members that made the loans were looking forward to being paid back, but instead they experienced difficulties. Sometimes this problem reached a stage where the food and beverage manager had to take the matter into his own hands. A smart gambler knew that today he promised to pay you back, and he knew that his next credit would die if today is pass.

Chapter-27

The crew member who took drugs was 100 percent a big-time problem to the company he worked for, the passengers he rendered the service to, and his fellow crew men that he worked with. The first thing about him was that he was not normal. He stayed hyper at all times. He was easy to upset. He was a complete problem maker to everyone. His top priority was to fight at the least provocation. His behavior was like a chuck around, a really big bully. He showed no respect to anyone, and he was always late for his job. Fluently he would use indecent language and never did his job properly. Because of drugs, he became very lazy. His appetite was open, and he consumed more food than the other crew members. Because of the addiction, he became a fingersmith. Guys from the east seriously loved to take drugs. It was like breakfast, lunch, and dinner for them.

There was a phrase out there that said "whatever it is that rocks your boat, go for it." I guess drugs were what rocked these guys' boats. All drugs were very convenient to the crew member who was in need. A crew member could buy any drugs on any island or in the States, plus he could buy them on board the ship from the guys who sold them. It was cheaper for the crew members to buy their drugs in port rather than on board the ship. But whenever their supply ran out, their need became so demanding that regardless of the drugs being more expensive on board, it was a must that they bought them. As late as the night was, and as deep as your sleep could be, you could be awakened by heavy knocking on certain cabin doors from blocks away or by the voice of one who cried in the night for drugs when he had run out and the shouting of the name of his drug colleague for help.

When a crew member was on drugs, it became very obvious to everyone. Especially if he just licked or sniffed cocaine, his attitude and motive told it all. First, he would report late, and his face looked shrunken. In his eyes was the look of a wild beast or a look as though he had seen a ghost. His hair needed to be combed; his uniform needed to be arranged and set neatly. Very often you would see him rubbing his nose. You didn't have to look too hard to notice that blood was running down from his nostrils. He was not normal in examining himself, and he did not know that his uniform was filthy. If the management consulted him about being late or about his appearance, he would get upset and not show any respect to anyone. On the job, he moved like he was running by battery and it was running out. Every fifteen minutes or so, this cokehead was missing, and when we found him, he would be on the stairway smoking, and then he would start to use the same indecent language to us again. Because he was constantly high on drugs, life had no purpose for him if he continued. Whichever department any drug addict worked in, the problem was the same. As soon as the cokehead ran out of money and needed to buy some more drugs, the assurance was that he was going to steal at the first opportunity he got, and there was no mistake about this. Knowing the rage that he was in, if anyone caught him alone and he realized that no one else was there as a witness to see him in the act, you'd better watch out,—a guy like this could kill you just to cover his tracks. Some of the things they did caused me to say life held no purpose or value for them. Most of the addicts, before they got hooked on drugs, had lives with meaning and values set to the course of success and happiness, until they failed to keep that integrity. Then their value and purpose in life made a complete full stop at the drain of doom. Their stereos, VCRs, cameras, good clothing, gifts, and other nice things that they bought for their families were now sold at a very cheap price. Stealing became a full-time habit in order to support their senseless need of drugs. For this reason, one who was under heavy drugs also seriously became a shoplifter, and oftentimes got caught because of his abnormal state of mind. Whether you were a drug head or not, once you got caught shoplifting, you were automatically dismissed from the company. Alcohol was not the problem, until one made it his or her personal habit to get drunk. Whichever word one seems fit to use, it is still one's constitutional right to have a drink, but still for all, one should respect his job. Personally, I loved to take a drink after work, knock myself out, nobody cared, I had all night to sleep it out. I could understand these guys more than anyone else. If one could imagine himself working thousands of miles away from his family across the globe, then he could understand that my personal experience as a seaman made me homesick sometimes. I did like everybody else would, I took a drink, but normally I did that after work. So what are the major things that caused these crew members to become alcoholics? I agreed that some naturally became addicted to alcohol because it first started out as a drinking habit, but for others it was just a part of the system and their state of mind.

The state that one's mind was in when he or she had just arrived was very weak, blind, and easy to break down. This system was different from the outside world. Men behaved like animals here, and with a new innocent mind, maybe you couldn't take the pressure whenever it came. Supervisors liked to give pressure to newcomers. The guys who were working there before you believed they owned the ship and had more rights than you did. Your cabin mate was going to tell you that he was in the cabin before you, so if you could not take the smoking, you were the one who would have to take a walk. If you were new, you should try not to be late for duty, because if you were, the first thing an ignorant supervisor was going to tell you was that if you could not come to work early and if you did not like your job you would be sent home with a one-way ticket. What made you know that this brain-damaged supervisor was picking on you was that he just talked to you about this and kept on repeating it while the old-timers came to work late, and nobody said a word to them. Your state of mind was still innocent and getting weak as everybody was on your case.

As a newcomer, you were blind to the fact that you should ignore some of these homeless, parentless, and futureless dummies, because this was not a place for a family man, especially if you thought about your wife really hard. The worst thing that could happen to a seaman was for him to receive a letter with bad news about his wife or girlfriend from his friends or family. This type of news could break down a man who was in love. On board the vessel, our best friends became the bottle and the pillow. When these things were happening to you, it became very obvious to everyone on the ship that you took up drinking full-time. During the service, one would go down to his cabin to have a drink because he had less than five minutes sometimes to go unnoticed. In every cabin, we kept hard drinks, which was against the rules. For the guys who did not have a problem, they still created problems by becoming regular drinkers on and off duty. Most of these guys never kept their jobs long. The worse complaints to the company were the ones that came from the passengers. The policy on all the cruise lines was for everyone to work against complaints, but some crew members just wouldn't quit. Too often complaints came in from the passengers about busboys and waiters approaching them with strong alcohol breath. Some dining room personnel stayed up all night partying, knowing that tomorrow bright and early their presence in the dining room was of great significance. Some crew members could not wake, while some came to work drunk from last night's activity. The head waiter who checked everybody who reported for duty would know when they were drunk or needed proper grooming. His duty was to send them back to their cabin to get themselves properly groomed, or if they were drunk, they would stay in their cabin until they became sober. Before lunch it was a must that they see the dining room manager in his office if he had one. For such an unprofessional and irresponsible behavior, this certainly called for an immediate dismissal, but if luck was on his side, this crew member would only receive a warning slip, which was one out of three.

Chapter-28

With the long years of traveling that I had personally experienced, I held no doubt in my mind that the fastest and easiest way for any kind of disease to transmit, especially venereal, was through the active movement of people from point A to point B. As long as people continued to travel from country to country and got involved in sexual activities, this case would get larger. Seeing is believing, and I was there. It really grieved me to see how rowdy and wild some passengers could get when they left their homes to take a cruise. The two groups who behaved the worst were the homosexuals and the ladies who cruised alone. Whether they were single or not, whether they came for the fun or not, eventually these ladies were going to run into a lot of young attractive men and their resistance would become very weak. It was a common practice for the crew members to change girls every cruise, and these crew members were very good at lying. They would say to any single lady, "Baby, you are the first passenger I've ever dated." Also, he would tell her that he had broken up a relationship a year and a half ago with his girlfriend, which was pure lies. Then again, who knows if she cared to hear about his previous relationship. If she wanted him, certainly she was going to tell him in her own way. As for the waiters, as soon as a lady sat down at his table, with the proper insight, right away he could tell that this woman wanted him really bad because all she ever did was keep on staring at him. The other passengers that sat around the same table that deserved attention and service hardly got the chance to talk or request something from their waiter, because of her. It normally happened that the waiters' and busboys' attention would be focused on the younger ladies or passengers rather than the older ones. Sometimes these young passenger ladies would be the last to leave the table because they purposely ate slow to kill some time. Before she got up from around the table, she would call the waiter over and ask him if he would like to join her in her cabin for a drink. No crew member was foolish enough to refuse such an offer, which was like daily bread to them. The real problem was, she did not know who she was getting involved with, and likewise, the waiter did not know anything about her. We had all kinds of people that took a cruise, and that was the reason why one had to take special precaution when dating. It was a fact that prostitutes did cruise with us frequently, and most of them were really beautiful and attractive. Still, it was a big chance one took without using a condom. Every night, whether in port or at sea, we would see the girls coming down the stairs to the crew cabins, and early every morning, you could see them going back up the stairs one behind the other. If two female passengers shared one cabin, and they were both involved with crew members, sharing the cabin would come to a mutual understanding, where they would give each other certain time for their pleasure. Some girls intentionally did it for the money. There were a lot of guys on board the vessel, and the thing that hurt me most was that these guys dated the passenger ladies every cruise. These bisexual men took the biggest risk concerning the spreading of disease.

During my twelve years of experience on board, I carefully noticed that the younger passenger girls from twenty-one to thirty, strictly and partially loved to date the mixed-nationality boys. Very few would date the Caribbean boys because the color of their eyes had no significance. But, the things beyond their knowledge were that they did not know the personal background of these guys who rejected the opposite sex. Another thing I noticed was that the older women in their forties still tried very hard to date these mixed nationalities and failed in doing so. These guys went for the younger ones and disregarded the older ladies; therefore, their attention was hereby avoided because of their age. During the whole cruise, these ladies would not give up trying until the last day of the cruise after they realized that they had not been seen or recognized by the mixed nationalities. That was the time we found them running to us Caribbean men for satisfaction, and that was one of the reasons why I for one continued to turn them down. The thing I said in my mind was, "Where was this woman when she was young, fresh, and green." Another thing I noticed was that these women didn't care who they went to bed with. Maybe they didn't have a choice. Maybe they were not getting enough attention at home.

Only the smart crew members watched out for the parents who traveled with their young daughters from fourteen to seventeen years of age, they purposely came to fulfill their money greed. The intention was to make money off the cruise line and to send some poor, innocent, and foolish crew member to jail. Some of these girls at age fourteen were very much overgrown. Some of these fourteen-year-olds had a boyfriend back home with whom they had active sexual intercourse, and their parents knew of their relationship, so they took the cruise in order to make problems. You would find a foolish crew member who would bite the bait. A girl at fourteen talking with the men and hanging out with them, would be missing for hour, and the parents would never try to find her because the plan was set. Once this little girl got all the information she wanted and the date and time was set, she would go back to her parents so that they could organize themselves for later. The move was between twelve midnight and one in the early morning, when most passengers and crew members turned in for the night. It was during these hours that the parents started to cry out for a missing child and stated to the officers that she always returned back to the cabin before midnight. Normally these young girls would tell their parents that the move was at midnight. She would tell them the name of the crew member she was going to be with, the name of the deck, and the cabin number. The parents then gave a grace period to make sure everything was in full order because it cost them a lot of money to come on the cruise and they couldn't afford to mess up this game of greed. At fifteen minutes past the hour, the parent would call the bridge to report the missing child and who she was last seen with, and then give the name of the crew member to the officer on the bridge with the security officer involved. When the report was made, they would take the name and find the cabin, and most of the time they would find both the girl and the crew member together. Without morals or dignity, the girl and her parents could not care less if this crew member had any form of disease or not. The security officer's job was to take the crew member into custody and wait for further notice from the captain. At the same time, the girl was brought before the captain and other top officers for an investigation where the young lady would answer all the questions. It was a must that she kept her story straight that John Doe invited her to his cabin. Either she told the captain she was forced to have sex or not; that was not of the parents' interest. They only wanted to know sex was involved because big money was coming their way. Disease was the least concern here. The girl who was seventeen years of age and mature and looked like twenty-one was another problem to the company and the crew. These girls normally told us that they were twenty-one and over; it was tricky. And it was all about sex, disease, and money.

Another active sex role that is between the crew for certain. I carefully observed this area. There was always more men than women on most ships. Normally when a female crew member newly joined the vessel and this was her first experience, certainly she would be confused from a competition of a men rushing to her. This was a moment in this poor and innocent girl's life where she had to pick choose and refuse; to play a vital role, She had to be very careful and lucky in chosing the right guy. If she accidentally chose the wrong guy, he would only use her for at least two weeks and then dump her. The rest of the crew would do the same thing because they did not get the first chance with her in bed. Now she was going to end up being used by half the crew on board by convincing her that the relationship would be steady. If she chose the right guy, things could be pleasant for her until the end of her contract when it was vacation time. For the lucky guy, things could turn out sour for him. Unfortunately, officers were part of the team also trying to impress this girl. Normally the female crew member preferred to date the regular crew members over the officers. Officers were too demanding and showed strong ownership and were tight with their money. A female crew member could also be demoted, transferred, or maybe get her service terminated if this psychopath officer held such authority. Once an officer decided that he wanted this girl, the most evil idea would be imposed on this person. If officers were not involved in this rat race, what I learned was that definitely as soon as one guy took his vacation, another guy would take over his place. There were times when a female crew member found herself pregnant and had to quit and go home to have her baby. Some crew members had a steady relationship and got married, although things happened between them. You would find the men trying to date other crew members and passengers, and the same went for the women. As the appointed time came for the first crew member to come back from his vacation, he was looking forward to taking back his girlfriend, and a fight could break out over her. If such uncivilized disputes occurred and the girl could convince her arriving boyfriend that nothing happened between her and the second, and if he should win her back, he had now become a big laughingstock on board. Fighting over a girl was an immediate dismissal from the company.

All the new girls learned very fast from the old ones. Their minds had been cultivated on both the ship's system and how to get around things. The men in general went bananas over the new employees, and that became very obvious to them. The smart ones would form a group and reorganize themselves purposely to take away money from the weaker men, especially if they were not working in a tipping area. For one to spend any short time with any of these girls during my earlier time on board, the cost would be fifty dollars, U.S. dollars, and up, and how weak one looked. This special group of girls made fast money and went home; some still hung around. The other group did not ask you for money. The agreement between these two parties was a weekly allowance plus the men would have to take them shopping. When it was time for these guys to go home, they were very broke. A week before vacation, they would stick up a poster on the notice board: items for sale. The other group of girls had to get a lot out of the men first. If she felt sorry for him, the opportunity for him to sleep in her cabin was just once in order to encourage him for more milking. Not one of these crew members thought of the possibility that they might catch any form of venereal disease.

Some officers had their lady friends cruising with them, and when these ladies walked around independently, they caught the attention of the crew members' eyes. Respectfully, if any crew member intended to get too friendly, his presence was no longer required on board permanently, but if she was popular with the crew, without any disrespect, the officers might run into some competition themselves.

Chapter-29

I have sailed to more than twenty-five different ports halfway across the globe. The Pacific Ocean, the Caribbean Sea, the Atlantic Ocean, and up the Alaska River, also from Quebec to New York. I have sailed across and above, the mysterious depth of the ocean that bore witness to and of the innocent and the guilty. A place that held many bodies of those who departed. A private cemetery for the wicked. A battle against justice. A place for destroying evidence. A place where evil held its foundation. This ocean, this same ocean, was the international gateway for death, destruction, pain, and suffering. The gateway of poverty and mourning, the weak and the strong, the greedy and the careless, the unwise and the blind. The gateway for those who were supposed to keep the law and the lawbreakers. A place for corruption and prosperity. It was an open door for all types of transactions. This open door created and cultivated a new breed of merciless, senseless, murderous generations that could not be tamed. Unfriendly and unjust were their daily prayers. Their thirst for vengeance was like a viper that sought its prey. Human love and feelings became a curse.

Automatically, without a choice and without any knowledge of my new environment that I was about to get familiar with, I became occupied with men and women who sought richies and glory in buying, selling, and trafficking illegal drugs which crippled the soul of mankind forever. Could illegal drugs stop? No. I didn't think so. Number one, illegal drugs have been exported and imported to various countries for medical research and were made legal in doing so. The question I asked was if any of these legal-illegal drugs hit the street. Secondly, narcotic forces were an embarrassment to intelligence concerning stopping drugs. Investigations seriously had to start from the top. Thirdly, why pay men to stop crime while some of these paid men were involved? I have seen many full-time narcotic operations on board the ship, and some of their operations were carried partially within. My drug education started in the early eighties when one of my cabin mates started to sell hard drugs and marijuana. As soon as the ship was docked, he would walk straight outside to the main street where he would take an unlicensed taxi to certain points and walk the last two blocks. Any intelligent person knew that undercover cops also drove taxicabs. Also no driver could be trusted; even if one of us got used to their faces, still they could be an informer for the police. A smart crew member could throw them off by letting the driver drop him at his girlfriend's house where he would spend one hour or two just to be on the safe side.

This illegal operation was for a cause. Because of a low utility salary, he had no choice than to put his whole future in the hands of the law if they caught him at any time. When he returned with the drugs, he would spend time to wrap them into small packages that made it easier to hand to his customers. At nights when we finished working, I would spend most of my time in the crew bar so he could have his privacy of supporting his customers' needs. When I couldn't stay up much longer, whether he was ready or not or liked it or not, I had to go to bed. In doing so, I had the opportunity to meet some of the guys I thought were straight. The Caribbean boys' cultural belief was that marijuana was the healing of the nation, which it was. My life was saved once because my father boiled marijuana mixed with other herbs sweetened with brown sugar and gave it to me to drink. Caribbean boys would come to the same cabin only to buy a joint to smoke while the other mixed nationalities loved to buy the hard drugs. Some nights it was difficult for me to sleep because the traffic got really heavy. My cabin mate was not the only one on board who sold drugs. There were others who did trafficking for other men, and the record was there to show that officers and passengers have been caught several times with illegal drugs. This was money we were talking about—the root of all evil. Drugs and money together became double evil. These two things took the lives of many, and who were the people that mostly got caught with illegal drugs? It was the people from the Caribbean and Latin America. The answer to these two problem was they were lacking money, and the only three areas on board the vessel that made fast money were the dining room, the bar department, and the cabin stewards. How would one compare these three tipping areas that made at least seven hundred dollars per week to those who made four hundred per month? It was a big difference. This was one of the main reasons why the fourth department, which was the utility department, got involved in drugs.

There were three ways that the drug trafficking could work. Either you bought it and sold it for yourself, or you could traffic it two ways: one for the guy on land and the other one for the guy on the ship. Buying and selling for yourself was very dangerous and not safe. How it normally was done was the person you bought it from on the island normally set up his police friends to bust you before you reached the ship. If you got caught on a lonely street, all his police friends would do was seize your drugs and let you walk. The crew member on board the ship; if he was hot with the police department he would pay another crew member to take his drugs off the ship in the United States port, but first, how easy and how hard was it to walk through the main gate full of security guards and narcotics police with their K9 dogs? With my experience and careful study I found out both the drug enforcement departments and drug dealers' secret. Every man had a price that made his clock tick. Once a man was involved, it was the hardest thing for him to quit. As all passengers and crew members made their first stop off with the intention to return without getting caught, only with good luck would one make it, and those who didn't would buy their way out. I believed this island was the worst of all other islands. Having a girlfriend on the island was an easier way to bring drugs onto the ship. This island was very small, and everyone actually knew each other. For this reason, driving through the main entrance to the dock had never been a problem because these guards never checked you like that. Drugs were not the main reason why these guards were at the main gate. They were there also to protect the passengers who got off the ship. The guards only stopped a car if it was not a taxi or if a crew member's girlfriend's face looked new in town. The guards would stop this particular car and ask the crew member to show his crew pass. If he was really a crew member, the car was allowed to drive through. If she was someone who knew the guard, hello was all it took, and they would never stop her. This same car, beyond their knowledge, would just pass through with lots of drugs. This kind of operation continued until a crew member foolishly blew his cover. Because of the same faces the guard saw passing once a week, the car would suddenly be stopped one day by a guard because he found out that there was drug trafficking going on, and he needed his cut. His home girl and himself would talk this out, and she would explain the condition to her boyfriend, the crew member. If he should disagree under the new condition, when walking or driving through the main gate, this crew member would be stopped and searched each time he entered the dock. If he agreed, he would be a rich man with only two people to pay: his girlfriend and the guard at the gate. The men that stood guards at the main gate were some times policemen. The guy who walked through with drugs in his possession was not wise and was taking a big risk with his freedom. The best time to walk past the guard definitely required a lot of patience. A clever drug trafficker would wait until the majority of the passengers were coming back from their tour and shopping. That was when the main gate would be crowded, and they must also carry a shopping bag in their hands and dress like a passenger. They knew that the guard never stopped passengers, neither for love nor money, because tourism was their only resource. Some of the unwise walked past the main gate and got caught when it was not crowded. But on occasion, crew members were able to run straight to the water and jump in, where they would destroy the evidence, but later be picked up by the water police for questioning. Crew members trafficking drugs were physically forced to outrun these policemen because most of them were very young. Some crew members used boats to carry them across, which was another way of entering the dock, for crew who have a police guardian would wait for him to be on duty. Independently, a crew member would wait until 2 to 3 in the morning when the guards were sleeping. Also, when you had a good friend as a policeman, his fellow police officers would leave you alone. Most of the big-time buyers would go to the casino to take a taxicab back to the ship. Guards never stopped taxis coming from the casino. Whenever a crew member was very heavy with drugs, he would take a taxi straight to the casino where he would sit and play for a while. He would look for passengers he knew from his ship. He would make sure to start a conversation with them and arrange for everybody to take one minibus back to the ship. They would pay individually, and each person would end up paying less than he or she normally would if he or she had taken a cab. No guard or policeman would stop a bus full of passengers coming from the casino. The passengers were the ones who trafficked the most drugs, and only a few foolish ones got caught. Only in Florida did they become unfortunate with the dogs sniffing their luggage.

Partiality sometimes played a major role in searching for drugs, and this was why I came to the conclusion that these policemen were the worst among all the other policemen of the islands and the least intelligent, and so are these narcotic police in the state. I have seen the way in which these men operate. The record can be shown that the majority of men that got caught with drugs were from the Caribbean and Latin America, because they were targeted. If I was a drug enforcing officer, millions of other nationalities would be behind bars. As we the crew members left the ship, every man and woman went his own way. On returning, only the men from the Caribbean got searched by the narcotics force. The mixed nationalities and others loved to play tennis. These certain guys would leave in a group to make it look like a big tournament was arranged between two ships. Later in the evening, upon returning, all that one could notice was just a group of sweaty men returning from a tennis match. Some of these guys were well loaded with drugs, and no guard at the main gate would stop them, not even for a crew pass.

I was stopped several times by the police and searched. They took me into a small room to do so. I felt very embarrassed, knowing that I did not do drugs. Why me? I turned to the simpleton and asked him, "How come you never search the other guys of mixed nationality?"

The simpleton answered, "You don't have to tell me how to do my job." It made me wonder how drug trafficking would ever stop when law enforcement officers were biased. Why didn't governments pay these guys more money? How foolish these people and their systems were. All the Caribbean men were behind bars, and none of them produced hard drugs. How could one stop a tree from bearing if he didn't pluck it from the root?

The rumor went around that another easy way for trafficking drugs was for a customs officer to bring it on the ship and another customs officer to receive it at the end of the cruise. All the crew member did was protect this merchandise until the customs officer arrived. The worst place to hide drugs was in your own cabin because if the dog found it, it would be a big problem for your cabin mates. If a crew member found out too late that the dog was on the ship and the drugs were moved, the dog could still know that there were drugs in the cabin. the would be noted by the narcotics police and would be closely watched on and off the ship. The ceiling in the corridor outside the cabin was a great place to hide drugs. Neither dog nor man have ever searched the ceiling. The toilet was another good place too. The dirty bucket with bleach water and mop was another area for hideouts. The kitchen, which we called the galley, was another great place for hiding drugs because it was a food preparation area where dogs were not allowed, and most of the time when the narcotics officer arrived, service was in session. The dining room was the best place to hide drugs. Who was going to enter a restaurant full of passengers enjoying their breakfast with a dog sniffing, which was prohibited? The bar usually closed on the last morning, and I never witnessed that area being searched. Also the movie theater that nobody went down to; the bridge, which nobody went up to; or the empty passenger cabins on embarkation morning, which was the last morning of the cruise—all the intelligent narcotics police could never once think that drugs could hide in these places. Cabins that were occupied by passengers could also be used for hiding drugs, especially when the passengers left their cabins to be cleaned. Crew members would hide drugs behind and under the dresser and in the ceiling. Narcotics police did not receive enough training on how to conduct a proper search on board a vessel. The only training they professed to me was storming the ship. The one place they usually ended up in was the utility area where the Caribbean and Latin American workers lived. Very seldom would you see them go into the mixed-nationality areas. Also, the cold storage was a perfect place for hiding such merchandise. All these hiding places I mentioned were never searched. If by chance they were, nobody would get the blame. On embarkation morning, I paid special attention to how the customs and police officers operated. Most crew members who carried in drugs would wrap them to their bodies. Mixed nationalities and Caribbean men did the same thing, but only the Caribbean men were searched. Because of that reason, the Caribbean men had to change their style of drug trafficking and studied the best way to take off their heavy burden that they had been experiencing with customs and narcotics police along with their K9 dogs. Now the narcotics police and customs could hardly catch anyone. Tight searches kind of slowed down, and the mixed nationalities had a better chance to traffic their drugs, but the best way to traffic drugs was............ No one would suspect you, and you could never get caught.

On board the vessel, we had another area that they called the shoot, which led straight to the bottom of the ship. A long time ago, the shoot would normally be used to dump food at sea. This shoot was an ideal hideout for drugs by tying the merchandise with a fish line long enough to reach the water. Some crew members would throw off their drugs early in the morning before entering the channel. These drugs would be picked up by some small craft.

After a period of time, some other crew members and myself were transferred to New York, where we would catch some other sister ship sailing down to Bermuda for six months. I had always heard of the Bermuda Triangle and how unpredictable the triangle water was. Today it would be calm and beautiful, and tomorrow, with a surprise, the water would get really rough. New York was a very nice place for shopping and visiting, but there were other cities that were less busy. The friendliest set of people that I observed here in New York were the ones who needed the help of a crew member and solely depended on the honesty of that crew member to traffic drugs for them. Honesty played a very big role in drug trafficking. Because the government was so hard on drugs, any crew member could sell his boss drugs, and when he returned with his boss's money, it was no big deal to tell your boss that the dog found the drugs. He would have to take your word for it when it was a dishonesty. Bermuda was the toughest place on drugs according to my studies in Bermuda. The dogs were always on the ship.

My transfer to a new environment to me was like graduating from high school and now entering college. As soon as the ship was docked and cleared, the moment we were finished working, every man was off the ship to his own order. There was this little bar across the street that only a few crew members visited to relax and drink. Nobody liked to stay on board when we were in port. Out on the street and inside the bar we could easily be recognized by both drug pushers and narcotics police; even the blind could recognize us. As soon as I approached the bar, a pusher confronted me. He wanted me to take drugs to Bermuda for him. I told him that I was sorry and that he should ask someone else. What I did not know was that most of the pushers trusted the new faces better, and it was kind of too early for the police to be watching the new boys. The old drug traffickers had gotten too smart with their drugs and money. I left him and proceeded to the other side of the bar with the thirst for some good whiskey. I carefully observed all movements but never tried to stand in anyone's way. This place was crawling with cops and drug pushers; even an arrest was attempted. Further up the same street, there was a little grocery store that we used to buy our liquor from. The crew would buy anything capable of hiding their drugs in. Some crew members returned with taxis while some walked. Every man to his own order. What I noticed in New York was that no one got searched getting on the ship. No questions were asked. On any ship entering New York, it was like Christmas for the crew because this was the best way for them to make some money. Every cruise when I returned to New York, the same guy would approach me again. In order to get rid of him, I said that I would see what I could do for him. He asked, "Like what?"

I said, "Just give me three months to study the dock people and everybody that moves on the waterfront, every bird that flies above the heavens, and every ant that crawls for crumbs."

He said, "That is too long." But still he could not fight my idea.

I said, "You speak wisely because I am the one would be caught in Bermuda, not you." On my way to Bermuda, there were certain cabins that the crew members used when stealing from their boss, once by once, from each package of hard drugs that they received from the pushers in New York before they delivered it on the island. There were a lot of crew members behind bars in Bermuda, and the majority of these crew members were from Latin America and the Caribbean islands.

Because the mixed nationalities and the passengers looked very much alike, customs and police at the terminal could hardly tell the difference between them. Also the mixed nationalities were very smart. They would exit the gangway at the same time with the passengers whenever they debarked in large numbers.

For many crew members who went down to Bermuda with drugs, the opportunity to return was not on their side because they foolishly became involved. As I had taken three months to learn the complete combination on how the police and customs worked, I now realized that I had to work my way around them very slowly because I had enough time to do so. I spent one month studying the customs and the customs rooms because the job on board the ship was very hard and the hours were long. The first thing I should have been doing after work each time was going straight to bed whether it was afternoon or night, but instead, I sat in the customs room just to observe everything that went on for the whole month. I now could tell who was coming on the next duty and whom I liked from whom I didn't, also whom I chose to chat with or not. I got friendly with whom I chose and whom I thought I could trust. I did get the opportunity to know a lot of policemen's faces and those in plain clothes. The best customs officer to have as a friend in Bermuda was a female, and it was not nice to rush to know her. Some of these ladies were intelligent and might think you had something up your sleeve. You always had to say nice things to the customs ladies and make sure you sounded more intelligent than they were. You could never ask her out on a date because that was not the purpose of getting to know her. If she began to like you, so would all her other customs friends. One thing I learned very fast in Bermuda was that the ladies went crazy over other Caribbean men. When both of us became very good friends, then it was possible for me to pass through the terminal without being checked. It would never cross her mind that I was trafficking drugs. After the first month had passed, I used the second month to study the undercover cops on the streets, also in the dockyard. As early as we arrived in the morning, there were cops heeling the dock men who were tying up the ship. A few small boats would be drifting in the dark hours of the morning pretending that they were fishing. During the days, you would see one of the madmen pushing one of those supermarket trolleys with garbage, pretending that he was mad. I watched him very carefully when he least expected anyone to be watching him. Suddenly he would reach below his garbage for his radio to report back to control. Some of the buildings across the street had a full view of the dock, the customs house, and the taxi stand. These buildings had empty rooms for the policemen's stakeouts. The containers on the dock at night were barely open and had a full view of the ship and the steps to enter the customs room. If any crew member was foolish enough to stop to rearrange any drugs in his possession, with one signal, a mountain of cops would suddenly surround him in the customs room. A crew member who got caught like this would not believe it because the way to the customs room looked very clear to him. Water police across the other side of the harbor in their speed boats constantly looked through their binoculars, hoping for someone to make their last mistake. Some of the taxi drivers were narcotics police, and I became very familiar with their faces. In any event that a crew member decided to take a jog because he believed in fitness, far behind him a policeman in short gear was also jogging and would watch him for the whole day. Each time I approached the gangway, on my left there were two narcotics policemen, and on my right there was one customs officer. If the customs officer found you with drugs, it was better to run and hide on the ship rather than run outside. The two policemen on my left were there to grab you if you tried to run, but if you were strong enough to flash past them, both the cops and the dogs would be looking for you. The third month I spent observing all the nightclubs, lounges, local bars, and shopping centers. From one nightclub to another, my night rest became more demanding of me, but that was something I had to overlook because my freedom meant more to me; my dream of raising a family would be in vain. Any man who was good at judging character could tell the difference between a civilian and a cop. These cops would sit and watch the crew while I sat and watched them. When a crew member was a suspect, the policeman's duty was to observe how much money he spent for each night and each day and during his shopping sprees. A crew member who had more than one girlfriend was also noticed. If one girlfriend was jealous because the other girlfriend got more attention, she would report him to the police. I was hurt to see these guys doing these things with no brains behind it. The cops would follow them during the day to the jewelry shops, where they would spend their money buying a lot of expensive gold chains and watches. How foolish one could get when he was involved—when he was doing something that was against the law. After I finished my three months' study, I then stood and talked with this certain guy in New York whose behavior was like the devil hoping for your soul to get to rot in hell. He couldn't care less if I got caught while trafficking his garbage into Bermuda. Doing so would be the first priority in his life. I would not dare sit with someone like this. At the end of the season, it was sad to me when I remembered all the crew members that I had left behind in prison.

As soon as I got transferred back to our regular route in the western Caribbean, I came to understand that there was a drug shortage in the western hemisphere of the Caribbean. There was this guy in Nassau who asked me if I had any connection in the States. He would have trust me with his money to purchase the drugs and traffic it back to him. He also assured me that he would have to pay me differently from the trafficking. That night he told me that the music in the nightclub was too loud and he wished to meet me next cruise and he would pick me up in person, which he did. While taking me to his house, I noticed the many turns he made before he reached his house. With the proper instinct, I said nothing to him. At his place, the unintelligent simpleton asked me to call a certain number in New York, which I had told him was the only person I knew of. By making this call, he would have the chance to speak person-to-person to organize the quantity and price before I started to do the trafficking for him. "No," I said, "that is not wise. Let me find out if he wants to talk with you first."

The man in Nassau said he would give it a try by calling him today. I still disagreed because I was sure this guy was a cop. The mistake he made with me was that he should have never asked me to make a New York call on his own private phone. This was unfair to the hundreds and thousands of men purposely set up with drugs by the narcotics police. After a while, I remembered a fellow crew member who got arrested for illegal drugs in the States. The narcotics force's idea was to let this guy stay on the dock to introduce money and drugs into some of us crew member's clean systems just to corrupt and poison us Caribbean men in order to put us away for a long time. I guess they enjoyed doing so. This convict had no choice but to ask us to buy drugs from him. The first morning I saw him on the dock, I thought he was free from his drug charges. There was one thing I was certain of, is that I respected him down to the very ground he walked on because he was patriotic enough to give his fellow Caribbean men a sign that the wicked were using him to catch us. What really hurt me was that the police were close by hiding in their cars. Therefore, this guy could not make a break for it. We all asked the question: Why did the evil ones always target us? I never saw one of these lowlifes, not even once, try to set up a mixed nationality.

Chapter-30

I am not an expert on shipwrecks or big disasters except for two experiences I have had. One was a tropical storm off the north coast of Puerto Rico from 10 PM that night until noon the next day. Still I would not want to find myself in that position again, although it was fun to me. And my second experience I had was that the ship ran aground, but I sat with other crew members that had personal experience with sunken ships in Alaska. I have seen minor fire on board before. It was nothing of great consequence to be panicked over. A shipwreck definitely kept one in suspense. One would be wondering if he would make it or not. A passenger ship could face disaster in a number of ways. Fire could be deliberately set by crew members, passengers, or terrorists. Once in a while, sea craft of all sizes and shapes ran into each other, or the bottom of the craft was ripped open by a reef. What type of wreck or disaster determined the speed of the sinking craft. It would create an atmosphere of panic, especially if physical injury occurred. All medical teams and officers were on their toes with one determination: to get the children, older passengers, handicapped, and injured out, which left plenty of room for vandalism and looting. The sunken ship in Alaska left the crew with only seven hundred dollars that they each received from the company for compensation of their personal belongings. Tragic incidences like these happened too fast for anyone to pay special attention to thieves. While passengers tried to reach the open deck, there were others with the intention to search the cabins and the main desk, where most of the values on board the ship were kept. But still, fire was our top priority to confront. Fire on board the vessel was not our biggest fear; it was the heavy smoke that prevented firefighters from breathing properly and getting the job done. It was the heavy smoke that blocked and trapped victims to their death. Crew members or passengers who smoked in bed were dangerous, and it was a senseless practice. On several occasions, a lot of crew members fell asleep in bed when smoking, but the rule for not smoking in bed went for both passengers and crew. It was more risky when an individual was under the influence of alcohol and fell asleep while smoking. It didn't matter how hard the captain preached over the P.A. system that no one should smoke on the open deck while the ship was refueling; you would still find a few crew members who thought that they owned the vessel, but with one flick of their finger, tossing a butt over the side where the barge was refueling, would certainly send us up into flames.

My experience with one tropical storm was a night to remember off the north coast of Puerto Rico. As we the crew normally did after working, we loved to admire the twinkling lights off the island while passing. At the same time, most of the crew would be guessing and naming the section of the island that they thought it was. We noticed that the wind and the swells were starting to act up. Shortly after that, the captain told the true story that we were heading straight into a tropical storm. All the officers on board now got busy that night tying up the doors that led to the open decks with ropes and securing and checking all portholes. The crew was ordered to clear the deck immediately. Every man, woman, and child entered his or her cabin and locked the door. It was senseless to most of us to lay down in our beds. Speaking for myself, I could not stay still. I got up and held on to the top bed while my cabin mate did the same. It was much worse for me and other crew members that night in our cabins. The waves kept us up right through the night. With a big bang on the ship, it sounded like we had just run over a big whale. The storm that night treated us like we were a piece of floating wood. Sometimes we went up, and sometimes we went down. We also rocked from one side to the other. Sometimes when the ship went down into the forward position, we all got the feeling that it was going down to stay. That was the part that frightened me the most. The midnight buffet was canceled since all the crew members were locked in for the night. It was beyond our knowledge how much damage took place within fourteen hours. Early the next morning, only a few crew members got up to check out their department. Most of the passengers and crew members were seasick, and the whole ship was looking and smelling like a hospital. The breakfast cooks could not make a move. No pots could stay on the fire even if they tried. On the open deck where the passengers walked around, water from the ocean came over on top and swept powerfully down the walkway. Luckily, all the doors were secured because the force of the water that came over would wash away any man or beast that stood in its way. It was near midday before the storm passed over and left us with a very rough sea that still tossed us around. It was later into the afternoon when we served coffee and sandwiches to the passengers because the cooks could not perform their duties properly. Later that afternoon, when things calmed down a little bit, all department heads assessed their damage. The storeroom at the bottom of the ship was in a big mess. Sealed containers with edible produce had burst open. Bottled drinks were broken, and all kinds of food were mixed up with each other. The complete storeroom underwent a complete repacking and cleanup. Not to mention the bar, which was a total wreck. The gift shop was also wrecked with clothing scattered all over the shop. They lost perfume, liquor, and other beverages. Breakfast and dinner plates were totally wrecked. The whole kitchen was in a disastrous state, and a few poolside chairs up on deck were washed into the ocean. Late that evening, the weather improved nicely, but a slight swell kept the ship rocking a bit. The kitchen team was able to start preparing for dinner.

The head chef was wise to prepare extra portions than he normally did. That night, nearly all the passengers on board ate an extra portion.

We the crew loved when any of these two disasters happened: one was a minor fire and the other was when the ship ran aground. Fire on board definitely caused discomfort to the passengers, and for this reason, the pool bar would stay open and drinks were free until further notice. That was where we the crew came in. This was the chance we had all been waiting for: to drink free and feel irie. Some crew members would even take a couple of beers and hard booze and hide it in their cabins. With so many free drinks floating around on the pool deck, the passengers now forgot that there was a fire. The firefighters could lose control if it got out of hand. Another disappointing time for passengers was when the sewage pipe burst and flooded out half of a section or a complete floor. Most of the time when the drainage system was blocked and started to back up into the cabins, the chief cabin steward and his team evacuated passengers from that area. The worst discomfort on board was engine failure in the middle of nowhere. On occasions like this, we could sit like ducks for hours without any electricity, only emergency lights to guide us to the open decks. Because of no air conditioning and the darkness, no one would want to stay downstairs. Since there was no electricity, this simply meant that the cooks were unable to conduct their duty, and the only thing the food preparation team could provide for the passengers was cold food, and we all had to live with that. After certain amount of time had passed and the engineering team failed to start the engine, the authority on board would arrange for tugboats to pull us to the nearest port or the main office would send one of the sister ships to transport the passengers back to the main terminal.

Regardless of bad weather at sea, whether it was rain or rough seas, the passengers always looked displeased and complained a lot throughout the whole cruise. They behaved so badly that most of the passengers failed to smile or pay back their respects whenever a crew member said hello to them. During the winter, a majority of the passengers that cruised on our vessel were from the north, leaving the bitter cold behind them, traveling south and searching for sunshine and expecting to return with a perfect tan. I was surprised to learn that most of these passengers had never seen the ocean from the day they were born. These were the kind of people that felt disappointed about the whole cruise when there was no sun or if the weather conditions hid the beauty of the ocean. Traveling to fulfill a dream became an experience filled with regrets and disappointment. All the sun worshipers on board had to clear the open decks and the poolside. The steel band had to stop their performance. The poolside bar sales dropped, and that was bad business for the bar department. The pool attendant now had the chance to stand with his hands folded and relaxed, waiting for nature to run its course. Passengers having their lunch on the open deck would bring their food to their cabins, where they would finish eating and leave the dirty plates outside their cabin doors. For some crew members, bad weather would lessen their work load, while there was an increase of work at other departments. Once the passengers disliked the outdoor conditions that nature provided, the dining room team would feel the pressure of a jam-packed dining room during the lunch hour, and that was bad business for the chef. He had to be very careful not to run out of items so he prepared less food on some dishes.

Under bad weather conditions there were two ports in the Caribbean that I had experienced where ships had to bypass and continue at sea or had difficulty entering: the channel in Nassau and Puerto Rico. The wind alone could cause severe damage to the ship, especially if the craft was small. When passengers became aware that they had missed one port that they had paid for, they became so rebellious to the crew instead of expressing their angry feelings to the management on board. They did not know that we the crew members were also mad about the bypass at any one of these two islands. These two islands were also our favorite spots, and a lot of crew members had plans for this particular day. Plus, this port was where some of us took our day off, and we were looking forward to it. I remember a different time when we had to sail from Los Angeles to Mexico with the expectation of entering four different ports, but we only had the opportunity to dock at one. Even though we were in port, a majority of the passengers stayed on board because of the weather. As soon as we set sail that evening, I was pleased to her an announcement made over the P.A. system that everybody would be getting a free cruise on the date of their choice.

Chapter-31

A passenger first step on the gangway serve them no sense of direction, for that purpose The management on board provided a welcome aboard team at the main entrance. This team was dressed in their special occasion uniform to direct the passengers to their cabins, the front desk, and other places. Any member of the team would also be happy to help bring hand luggage if it was heavy or if there was more than one piece. Some of the passengers would ask us straight away, "Where is lunch being served?" If any information they sought seemed above the team member's head, one member of the team would direct the passenger to the information desk, where their question would be answered and their curiosity would be satisfied. While the embarkation of the passengers continued, the bar team rendered their services and provided a welcome aboard mixed drink at a minimum charge. Also in one of the showrooms a welcome aboard performance of music was provided by the crew staff along with a welcome aboard talk. In the meantime, the steel band would be playing their welcome aboard island music. Lunch or snacks may have been provided on board for passengers, depending on which cruise line it was. As long as the embarkation continued, the photographer would stay outside the terminal to take the first picture that would bring back memories for a lifetime. While the talk show continued, the cruise director would introduce all his staff and explain everything in full detail about the ship. As the minutes passed by, half the passengers on board were getting ready for dinner. The beauty salon was another area that became busy with the ladies who were trying to re-fix their hairdo on the first day. After dinner was over, it was show time, and no one needed to stay in their cabin and get bored with so many activities going on, unless one really felt tired. Cable movies and all-day ship movies were in each cabin; plus, a multi-programming channel for music and talk shows was provided inside all the cabins on the ship. Every night the cruise director would program a different show in the showroom for the passengers. On some lines, the first night started out with dancing performed by the ship dancers. A comedian and a magician would take their turn. Also, they were impersonators of famous superstars performing in the showroom. There was always something on board to keep the passengers occupied. The gift shop on board the vessel was not a large one compared to those in the mall on shore side, but it still provided a wide variety of inexpensive and attractive items that enticed one to spend. The shop was open from 6 PM on the first evening after we set sail and closed before midnight. Passengers always left a few items home that were necessary on their trip. Whatever that item was, they could purchase it in the gift shop. The disco on board was also open for the dancing pleasure of the passengers including the lounge and several bars in different locations. At midnight, the buffet either on the pool deck or in the dining room was open for the passengers' dining pleasure after a long active night whether it was dancing, watching the movie, or drinking. After midnight, the casino just picked its form, while some passengers were winning and others were grieving over their losses. All this and more took place in just one night. On some cruise lines, room service was available to the passengers who believed in a lot of privacy, especially for the honeymooners. This kind of service was to the advantage of passengers who hung out late at night or to those who were definitely late risers. To call home and say hi to the family was easy but expensive. Personally speaking, I only made calls on special occasions.

At six thirty in the morning, early bird coffee was ready for the early risers. As the new day approached only the weather provided by nature could turn the blue sky into grey. If the sky was blue and the sea was calm, all regular scheduled sports and other activities would proceed as planned during the cruise. All these activities would take place, such as table tennis tournament, golf, trap shooting at the extreme back of the ship, swimming, poolside bingo, and poolside horse racing. Every morning before these activities began, one member of the cruise staff would lead the walkie-tang group up on the top deck in to shipshape condition. So many times around the deck would be the equivalent of one mile. Music by the poolside went on all day played by the steel band, while the sun worshipers stuck to their daily constitution. Passengers danced half-naked to the beat of the drum, while young ladies made winding movements to the tune of the music in front of the band. At noon each day, the navigation report from the bridge would announce, and the reporting officer would also give the weather update. Some time later into the afternoon, an international wine-tasting seminar would take place in one of the lounges. The wine was accompanied with a wide selection of cheeses. During the cruise, the gift shop would also perform a seminar to help boost their sales. Step aerobic fitness classes were directed by one of the crew staff. There were so many things to do on a cruise. A cruise could be fun if one left his or her home problems behind. There was also a wonderful dance lesson for passengers who loved dancing. It was hard to tell what passengers were doing on the dance floor. From my point of view, it looked like they wanted to hit each other, and the way they tossed their heads around, a good dancer might pick up a head butt that left one unconscious. The beauty salon and massage therapist were open daily. Free poker and napkin-folding lessons were also provided by the crew. Before the day was over the welcome aboard picture taking was ready to be picked up in the photo gallery, but not all passengers could afford to pay for it. The tour desk was open all day for any passenger who wished to purchase a tour ticket for the next day when we arrived in port. Also the cruise director would hold a very interesting travel talk on all the islands and how to spend-bargain, and say that it was much cheaper taking the tour that the cruise line provided than doing it independently. The passengers would be informed to the maximum about the people, what they should expect from them, and whether it was an English-speaking country or not. They would be informed about the currency rate, the best shopping areas, and how much it would cost to travel from point A to point B. Once per week, the captain would invite all passengers to his cocktail party. At this reception, party champagne and hot and cold hors d'oeuvres were served. Picture taking would take place with the captain at some point with the passengers. To accommodate all the passengers at the captain's reception party, we would divide the passengers into two sessions. The first seating party would start at 5 PM and be over just before 6 PM. Dinner was then served at six, and between six fifteen and six thirty, the second seating party for passengers began while the first seating party was just eating their dinner. Before the cruise had come to an end, the master of the vessel would have a repeater's party for people who had cruised before. At least five to six top officers had their personal table at which they dined. These tables carried six to eight seats, except for the captain's table, which held ten to twelve seats. These top officers liked it when the booking team assigned younger ladies to their tables, an age group not over forty.

Chapter-32

There were many cruise ships out there, and they all carried different-sized styles and shapes. It was a competitive world that sought to build a reputation on their names so that their foundations stayed firm and tall. The architectural structure was built with such unique and glamorous beauty that trying to resist the temptation was futile. A large fleet covered the ocean floor with multiple colors to choose from. The capacity of a vessel was determined by its size and its weight. A small ship with a length of under seven hundred feet and a weight of nineteen thousand tons should carry up to eight hundred passengers and under four hundred crew members. A midsize vessel under nine hundred feet in length with a weight of under forty thousand tons should carry under one thousand five hundred passengers and a little under six hundred crew members. The larger ship with a length of over nine hundred feet and a weight of about eighty thousand tons should carry under two thousand five hundred passengers and about one thousand five hundred crew members. Most companies were now building their new ships under one pattern and color for a better identification for themselves and others near or far. But if your experience should put them all on one scale, their beauty and a well-designed structure would carry no value if the general crew was not genuine in everything they offered and what the cruise line portrayed. It was a competitive world that tried to be pleasing in all aspects of hospitality that would be well taken by their customers. These companies were wise. As I saw for myself, they were composed of employees who, combined, spoke more than twenty-five different languages, trying to break the barrier of communication with the passengers who cruised with us from various parts of the world and were in need of information about what to do, where to go, and their new environment. It would be very embarrassing for a cruise line that catered to an international interest to fail to converse with or interpret for their guests. Another excellent move that I have recognized was the complimentary champagne that was distributed in the cabins for repeater guests by the cruise line. Wine and champagne were presented to the passengers at dinnertime by their wine steward, which was a surprise gift from their travel agent. It was possible to have flower arrangements from the flower shop on shore side delivered straight to the cabins. Whether it was for a sentimental reason or not, nothing was better liked than when a crew member was possessed with a good personality and offered friendly service, especially the dining room staff. A beautiful smile and a wonderful welcome was all it took—then to pull the chair out and pull the napkin before introducing the menu. Because these lines provided for a wide variety of passengers, you would find the food there was exceptional. Every night passengers would experience a different dish of a different nationality prepared by their favorite chef. I must confess that people who did not have quality taste would complain about the food.

Chapter-33

My third dry dock experience took me to Baltimore 1995 in winter. This was my first visit to this city. I had heard so much about Baltimore from tourists who had visited my island. Going to Baltimore was like a dream come true. Two days on sea were worth the trip. Every time I visited the open deck, the temperature got colder due to the course that the navigating officer set. Luckily for me, I had my winter jacket and some thick socks. The dry dock in Baltimore was a very large one, but still we all had to wait until other ships left the ramp before we could go in. Leaving hot, sunny Florida and suddenly ending up in this super-cold place, my body did not adapt to the change of climate fast enough. I happened to catch a very terrible cold that caused me to believe I would not live out the first week. The air conditioning on board the ship chipped out sometimes and caused the inside of the vessel to be hot. The upper deck of the ship was full with crew members trying to escape the heat below. After a good twenty-five minutes looking around and admiring the frozen river and the bridge that took the traffic across it, I started to feel different in my body, so I proceeded downstairs to my cabin and lay down for a while. That same night I did not leave my cabin for any reason whatsoever.

On the third day of the month, I was awakened by a loud knocking on my cabin door. I was told that it was a bad practice to lock your cabin door when sleeping, so I just closed it. When the person entered the cabin, I recognized that it was the wake-up man. He was a dining room waiter. It was his job to wake all the dining room personnel in order for them to be on duty at the specific time required by the company. It was seven fifty five in the morning, and we only had five minutes to be present for the roll call that took place in the dining room by one of the head waiters.

Now I turned into the fourth day of the month and around 9 AM that morning I noticed that whenever I bent down to do anything, my head hurt badly and beat heavily like a drum. By midnight I started to feel worse. I never put much of this to mind. By 6 PM that evening, I went straight to my bed because I was not feeling right within myself. While I was in bed, I recognized that it was fever and flu. I asked my cabin mate to bring me some hot black coffee because I needed it to mix with some white rum that I purchased on one of the islands. I tried this simple remedy, but it did not help me. At 10 PM I was awake and feeling very sick. In my sickness, I believed that it was 10 in the morning, but I was wrong and still did not notice it. I went up to the dining room that night to report the matter to the maitre d', but the restaurant was empty. I then believed that everybody was on coffee break and still believed that it was morning. I was too sick to realize it was night. I was very weak, and I had to pull a chair and sit for a minute. My body hurt all over, and I was experiencing a painful headache along with joint pain. My ribs hurt, and my throat was sore. I could not wait any longer for the maitre d' to come down to the dining room so I decided to call his cabin. It was beyond my knowledge that I awakened this man from his sleep. He eventually answered the phone after several rings, and I finally got the chance to explain my condition. I also told him that I visited the doctor's office and he was not there. The maitre d' said okay, so I thought he was coming down to see me. Since I was waiting too long for the maitre d', I decided to call the bell desk and ask them to get in touch with one of the nurses on duty, which they did. The nurse called and asked me what the problem was. I told her the symptoms that I was experiencing. She asked me when I last ate something. Yesterday, I answered her. She told me to come back in the morning. I was so sick that I told her it was impossible to wait any longer. She said, "Let me call the doctor and get back to you." After a while, the phone rang, and I answered it. She told me that the doctor said I had to go up to the bell desk and ask them for some Tylenol and see him in the morning. I couldn't believe this. Nobody would help me. Why? After I received the Tylenol, I went back to my cabin and took two. I could not sleep through the rest of the night. By five o'clock, I fell asleep.

Fifteen minutes to eight that morning—this would be the fifth day—I was awakened by my cabin mate. He asked me if I was going up to the dining room for the roll call. "No," I told him, "I will be seeing the doctor." That morning I could barely get out of my bed. I tried very hard to climb down the ladder that led to the crew mess. I tried to eat something or drink a cup of hot tea, but my throat was too sore to do so. The crew visiting hours were at nine thirty AM, but I was fifteen minutes early, so I sat down on one of the steps that led directly to the dining room. Not long after, I saw the dining room manager coming down the stairs. He passed me sitting down on the stairs, and he did not say anything to me. I did not know if he recognized me or not. Shortly he went up the stairs again and said nothing to me. Coming down the stairs again, he looked at me and asked why I was not at the doctor. I pointed my finger toward the clock and showed him the time; it was five minutes before the doctor's office opened. He did not state any word about me calling him last night, and he did not ask me how I was doing. At 9:30 AM, I went to the sick bay. I happened to forget to fill out an authorization form, and the nurse asked me for it. "I did not find my department head," I answered.

"Next time you should bring one," she said. Nothing she said to me at that moment meant anything because I was too sick to chase my department head all over the ship to obtain an authorization form. I felt like death was knocking on my door. My temperature and blood pressure were checked by the nurse. After that, she told me the doctor would be here shortly. Half an hour later, still the doctor did not show up. The sick bay started to get filled with patients, so the nurse decided to call the doctor in his cabin to find out if he was on his way. To our surprise, the doctor was still in his cabin, and the hour for his presence was overdue.

I heard the nurse ask the doctor over the phone, "Are your kids coming today?" and then she hung up the phone.

It was now five past ten in the morning when I saw the second nurse enter the office. She knew me by name and asked, "What happened to you?" I repeated to her what I had told the former nurse. She called me into another room and gave me three different types of tablets to take. One was an antibiotic, Keflex 500, and the color was red. The amount given to me was twenty tablets. She said I should take one capsule four times per day. The second tablets were ibuprofen, 800 mg and a total of nine tablets. I had to take one every eight hours after meals. The third tablets were acetaminophen, 500 mg and a total of twelve tablets. I had to take two tablets every six hours. After a split moment, she crossed out every six hours and put every four hours. After doing so, she told me to return the next morning. Now that I had started to take these tablets without a doctor's advice, I took them right through the day as was prescribed. It was almost midnight, and none of these tablets seemed to be working.

I was awakened in the morning by my cabin mate again. He asked me, "You think you can make it to work or not?"

"I will try," I answered.

He said, "Okay, I am leaving." Then he left and closed the door behind him. My cabin had an inside bathroom so I didn't have to walk far like on the other ships. Before my cabin mate left, I remembered he warned me not to take a shower so I dry-cleaned myself and paid the sick bay another visit. The doctor was in his office that morning. "Thanks be to God," I said to myself.

The nurse told the doctor about me so he called me in and asked me what the problem was. I repeated myself for the third time. Because I did not make any changes, the doctor looked at me as if the nurse was doing something wrong to me. Assisting the doctor that morning, she looked down my throat. After I told her my throat was still sick, the doctor asked her how my throat was. No answer came from her. Then the doctor looked for himself and said it was very bad repeatedly. He said, "I am going to change your tablets." He gave me a set of new tablets and gave me two to take right away right in front of him. The nurse gave me a cup of water to take these tablets with. Then the doctor told me to sit down and let these tablets take effect on my body before I took another set of tablets after three minutes. The nurse told me within one hour I should take one tablet every twelve hours and come back the next morning to see the doctor. Sweet Jesus. From 9:30 AM until 2 PM still I didn't feel any better. Anyway, I went to bed that evening and woke up at 4:30 PM the next evening, feeling hungry. I made my way down to the crew mess and waited until 5 PM before the line was open. The crew mess was very cold because the air conditioning was on. The food line was now open, and I made my way to the front of the line. I took a small portion of food without meat or gravy because I had lost my sense of taste and I could hardly swallow. I then proceeded to my cabin where I tried to pass the food down my sore throat to fill the space of gas that started to give me gas pain.

It was eleven days on the ship before I stepped off the gangway to make a call home to my family and another two days before I visited downtown Baltimore. It was snowing on and off all along. On my way out of the shipyard, there were other crew members up ahead of me. As we stopped at the guard room, which was the main gate, we waited there for the buses and the taxis. Everyone was crying out that their butt was freezing off. We then decided to walk to the next guard room where some other crew members where being sheltered against the bitter cold. The guard called us in to the shelter with the others and called a couple of cabs for us. When the cabs arrived, the group went in two separate cabs. It was like a tour to us because it was our first time to the Baltimore dry dock. I remember that I passed three cemeteries, and the third one was in the bushes, in what looked like a forest for wildlife. I asked the driver of the cab, "Who is buried here?" He answered me and said that only the African Americans were there. Right away, emotionally, I was turned off by everything because whatsoever atmosphere I see or feel that is what the people represent like wise other town and city I have been to. I could not share my true heart in a house of madness.

Chapter-34

Taking a cruise along any route of your choice could certainly become an unhappy voyage if one was not fully informed about the cruise line that he or she was about to book on. Older folks probably should cruise on a line with people of the same age group, although some older folks look and feel young. Every cruise line I knew of set up a daily program according to the type of crowd they carried. A family cruise line should be the recommended line for families, small or large. There were other attractive cruise lines that families were really anxious to try just for the experience of it, and I saw nothing wrong with that. The type of programs that the family cruise staff organized for the kids on board definitely would stay in their memories for life. To attract mostly kids, some family cruise lines would use cartoon characters to uplift the spirits of both children and parents by having these characters play, give autographs, take pictures, and have a whole lot of fun. On board these ships, there was a group of reliable kid counselors that were in charge of all activities such as kids tours, birthday parties, talent shows, cartoon characters, and tuck-in service at night, as well as babysitters for parents who wanted to go and see the night shows on the island whenever we spent overnight in port. Also, there was a large games room for kids of all sizes and ages. Breakfast with the characters on some of the mornings made the families feel very special. Because this was a family cruise line, kids were all over the ship. They ran from one floor to another. They knocked on almost every door, looking up their friends. Disturbing your neighbor would go unnoticed, and for those who felt disturbed, we would keep hushed because their kids were involved. The elevator on board the ship played a vital role.

Where older passengers were concerned, some were not strong enough to climb the stairs and complained after waiting too long for the elevator. It was a pain in the neck after waiting to find out that all the buttons in the lift were pushed and it had to stop on every floor. Older folks simply should avoid spring break cruises unless they chose to do so. Spring break was a very active moment on board, which was worse than regular family cruises. These grownups were very energetic and took a lot out of anyone who decided to keep up with them.

If anyone is planning a trip and looking forward to finding peace and quietness, I would suggest to their agent that the passengers be fully informed and let the passenger make the decision which one of the cruise lines he or she wanted to be the cruise. Taking a cruise is a very great idea, depending on which line you choose and how much it cost you to be on board, also how much the cruise line has to offer you for your money. Service should be the number one objective, although the main complaint on most cruise lines is their food. Booking a cruise with bad timing certainly can spoil all of your expectations. Hurricanes and bad weather such as a cold front that affects the Bahamas, the Pacific, and the northeast section of the Caribbean waters can make a rough ride possible. Under these conditions, one cruising for the first time can easily become seasick, although some repeating passengers also still feel seasick. Because of a cold front, most of the islands that are the closest to the United States have less sunshine available for the sun worshipers, and there is a 60 percent chance of rain.

Officers or cruise staff, whichever one seems fit, should be more informative over the P.A. system about some of the islands' historical background each time they pass one closely. Such initiative will cultivate the minds of both passengers and crew. Finding some of the islands less attractive than expected can also ruin some passengers' cruises, especially if there is less to see or do. Whether it is family, honeymooners, or any special occasion, while one chooses to take a cruise, he or she must remember one thing: try to adjust himself to his new environment and let the natural vibes flow, because if one fails to do so, his or her money is not used wisely. While being at home away from home, and whether one likes it or not, every single person aboard the vessel happens to be one big family and should be very proud of it because out there every man's life is in each other's hand.

Air conditioning is another area that can cause discomfort to passengers. It is a fact that not everyone can live with the same temperature, but the complete interior of a vessel needs a proper air conditioning system to separate the heat and transform your new environment into a temperature that is pleasing and relaxing. On board a cruise ship, all cabins carry a switch to control the temperature to your likeness. There are cabins that we call the inside cabins. All out-side cabins carry a porthole that can be opened if you care for some fresh air, or for passengers who do not keep good health in an air conditioned system. These porthole are also excellent for viewing other vessels passing by and whenever passing some beautiful island nearby, instead of viewing it from one of the open decks. There are cabins that are located in certain areas of the vessels in which the engine room can be heard and this becomes very disturbing on some ships, especially the older ones. That can cause restless hours to passengers, whom I have served and shared the same experience with, in the past as a busboy. If anyone should unfortunately happen to experience this in the future, it is possible for a cabin change if the vessel is not full to its capacity. Passengers who are assigned to a table that they dislike can have an unenjoyable cruise. This one table alone can be interpreted into multiple discomforting areas. Too often I have served passengers with large families who requested that they would like to sit together. Unfortunately, not all requests can be granted. It all depends on how the dining room was designed. In some of the ships' restaurants, the tables are firm to the floor. If these tables were moveable, passengers would have the right to express their unsatisfied feelings if their request were not fulfilled. Not many tables for two are inside the ships' restaurants, although some ships carry more tables for two than others do. I agree that most couples prefer to sit by themselves due to a private affair. Not everyone would like to share their personal life with others. Outside agents normally make errors when placing reservations for passengers of two and request for them a table of two, which is limited. Outside agents should know in advance whether or not a table for two is still available. Passengers that are assigned to a table often share with other passengers of a different nationality. Religion or culture should be aware of the fact that these assignments are possible.

As a waiter on board these vessels, I served two different groups on many occasions, and because they did not like each other for whatever reason, sometimes for the whole cruise, these passengers did not speak to each other. If one group noticed that the waiter was serving the other group first, each time that the waiter approached the table it was guaranteed that the waiter's tip would be decreased and there was a possibility for a bad markup on his rating sheet.

Passengers booking their cruises either with the main office or an outside agent must remember to inform them about their health problems. Frequently I have served passengers on my table with no knowledge that they were diabetic or vegetarian, etc. I believe that passengers who have to travel with their medication should properly inform someone and see whether or not they can receive the same medication on board if they run out.

On a cruise ship, the most delicate area to feel and to be satisfied with is the food. The food that is provided on board is not any form of a native dish but cooked in an international way to please everyone. Some items carry MSG. Because of the ingredients the chef uses to make the dish tasty, sometimes passengers do get turned off by tasting a dish that looks delicious, even if that dish carries an excellent presentation. For this reason, it is the policy of the dining room to exchange any dish that the passenger chooses from the menu. Refusing to do so can spoil the day or a complete cruise for the passenger.

I have seen passengers receive burns from the sun on board so bad that they had to visit the ship's doctor. In port they would love to go on the tour that is on the program but deprived themselves of such an opportunity, and such disappointment could cause them not to appreciate the remainder of their cruise. Sun worshipers should be informed about lying in the Caribbean sun, especially when they are on sea, when the weather is calm and not a wave is to be seen, neither any breeze to be felt blowing in between the heat. This can cause a terrible burn if their skin is too sensitive for the ocean sun. So, bringing your favorite suntan lotion would be wise. The gift shop on board by chance might not have the type you wish to use.

Passengers complaining about the crew before the cruise has ended are not wise because if that individual knows about the complaint, the genuine service will disappear, and this is not what you pay for. Some passengers are very clever by writing the company from home and explaining their problem in detail. This way, the department head cannot and will not have the opportunity to cover up for one of his favorite staff members. On occasion, passengers do sail off, leaving their luggage behind them. Certainly such a mistake can start the cruise badly. I have seen passengers stay in one suite for more than two days, but most of the time their luggage would end up in a different cabin and would be later discovered and returned to them, the rightful owners. I missed one piece of luggage once after debarkation at the airport. I delayed too long when I should have proceeded right away to pick up my luggage first. On the other hand, the company address and the name of the ship should be also on the passenger's address tag. This way, the cruise line can fly a passenger's luggage over to the first port the ship stops at.

At any port of call, not all the passengers will choose the tour that is arranged by the cruise line. Most of these passengers will walk off independently. One thing that I am certain of is that the tour that the cruise director has on the program is cheaper and safer. Independently, if any unlicensed taxi operator outside the dock convinces a passenger to have them shown around, positively the passengers will see more, but upon returning, the trip can be unaffordable. If passengers believe that they have been robbed, this incident along with others can help spoil their cruise.

Chapter-35

If I could have seen the future, I would have avoided a serious problem that I am now experiencing. My health took a different course unexpectedly, causing me to live on medication until who knows when. These persisting symptoms will not stop so that I can live a normal life like others do. I cannot do much walking or lifting due to injuries I received while working in the dining room on board the ship. My injuries were caused from lifting heavy trays both with food and dirty dishes back and forth to the kitchen. Most of the time, I had to help out my busboy by carrying out his dirty tray with lots of dishes to the dishwasher so I could reset in time before the doors were opened for the second seating. I did this a lot, especially if my busboy had a large station and two to three waiters that he was assigned to. Some busboys were very slow, while some were lazy. Working on a cruise ship called for hardworking people, and I was one of them. Dancing in the dining room every week during the Caribbean night dinner really made me more tired than any other duty that I had ever performed on board, because I had to dance right around the dining room so that all the passengers could enjoy the show. There were thousands of pictures of me around the world. Dancing was not in my contract, and as an excellent dancer, I tried to hide because the dining room manager or head waiter was looking for me. The Caribbean show was not a show without we the Caribbean men dancing up front with the fire on our heads because none of the other nationalities could do this in a perfect way. For us to dance in the front was very demanding and pressuring. More often we crouched very low on the floor in order to look our best, especially for picture-taking.

This night was going to be the last night of my dancing limbo style. It was April 1995 when I made my final limbo crouch. Suddenly I felt like something pulled in my left knee. It hurt so badly that while trying to get up on my left knee, I couldn't take the pressure. I finally got up. I happened to hop-dance my way across the remainder of the floor. As the week passed by, I still continued to dance but avoided doing the limbo style. On and on, I did not pay any special attention to my left knee until I noticed that whenever I started to climb the stairs, the upper right side of my knee became very painful. I went to the ship's doctor a few times, and I received some medication that did not help me.

On the 17th of October 1995, I went back to the ship's physician, and I was examined and treated for something he called tendersey in the knee. The doctor also showed me a chart with a picture of a knee with two veins. He said that at my age I should not be bending as far down as the younger men do, so I might have strained them. The follow-up care on board the ship did not show any improvement. The ship's doctor set an appointment for me to see a shore side doctor provided by the company. I remember he ran some x-rays and told me that nothing was wrong with my knee, but still he gave me some medication to take. I now realized that none of their medications were helping me, so the shore side doctor set an appointment for me to see a rheumatologist. He also did not find anything wrong but gave me a prescription to pick up, some Voltareen to take for one month and to be refilled for another month. Each prescription contained one hundred tablets. The doctors' orders both on shore side and on the ship were that I must stop dancing, the remarks coated, must not crouch, must not dance limbo, and must avoid climbing stairs.

The seventeenth of October 1995, I went by the front desk and asked one of the bellboys to photocopy the crew authorization medical form. I was supposed to keep one copy for myself and surrender the other form to the dining

182

room management. The assistant maitre d' said, "It is okay. Since you are sick, there are other Caribbean boys who will dance." I remember that I was having a short talk about my dancing with the dining room manager and for the first time in my waiter-dancing career, a member of management really looked me in the eyes and told me I didn't have to dance and nobody was forcing me. This was one of the biggest hypocrites I was ever confronted with. In some companies, the management moved around from ship to ship, and it was not bad working with this maitre d', although none of the maitre d's was my favorite. Everyone had their ways; we just had to get used to them. The new maitre d' that signed on the ship was the least respected by the men because his time on board was over due to his age. Most older men's ideas stayed with them. We the younger men believed in new ideas plus the new maitre d' was trying to gain respect through bull force and unfriendliness.

As the weeks passed by, he somehow noticed that I was absent from the parade which was the Caribbean dance. He did not wait to tell me in person that if I missed any of the parades again action would be taken. So he called all the dining room staff for a short meeting and explained himself. The following cruise I decided to join the parade line even though my left knee was not healed as yet. During the main seating dinner, I joined the parade line in order to avoid the maitre d'. While I was dancing, one of the head waiters tried to pull me out of the line aggressively and told me that the maitre d' wanted to have a word with me now. At the end of the parade, I told the head waiter. Whether he understood me in the big noise from the parade or not I couldn't tell, but one thing I knew was that the head waiter returned to the maitre d' with something different from what I said. At the end of the parade, I approached him to see if he was feeling any pain because I did not dance with the fire, which was the doctor's orders. Dramatically he said, "Go see the chief steward in his office." He was only trying to embarrass me.

I knocked on the door of the chief steward. Someone answered, "Come in." As I opened the door and looked, who was it? Nobody but the newly promoted chef. He asked me why I was not dancing. I told him the real reason. He looked at me with a merciless heart and said, "The show must go on," and if I refused to dance during the second seating, he would have to sign me off the ship at the end of the cruise.

I said, "Sorry, sir, it is the doctor's order."

The chief steward said, "Okay, you leave me no choice. I will have to sign you off."

On the last night of the cruise, I received a sign-off form stating I would be transferred to another company that sailed out of Montreal to New York. I only spent one week there because my presence in the dining room as a colored man was not appreciated. The moving around of the dining room maitre d' frequently move around from ship to ship simple because we work for a concessionaire.

After rejoining the original company in Florida, they did not send me back on the previous ship that I had my dancing problem with. I was signed on to one of the other sister ships. This was in October 1995. On board, I continued to dance the first cruise, trying to avoid another sign off because I needed to work and support my family. During my second cruise, I failed to dance because I put too much strain on my left knee, which was injured. I complained to the dining room management about my condition, and they told me to give the dancing a break, which it was too late for. Deep down inside their hearts they wished a star like me would never be sick.

I remember quite well that the treatment of my left knee stopped when I was sent to Montreal, and when I returned in one week, the follow-up treatment was discontinued in

October 1995. I started to experience a pain in my left wrist caused by the tray I had been carrying with food also, when I returned the tray to the dishwashers with the dirty dishes. Inexperienced at that time, I thought it was a simple strain, so I started to put most of the weight on my shoulder. I realized that doing so did not help the left wrist condition.

When back in the main port, I caught a cab to town because the town was quite some distance away. I purchased a hand support that carried some kind of steel in the center of it to bear the weight. Acknowledging too much pain caused me to pay a visit to the ship's physician. After the doctor finished examining my left wrist, he offered me another hand support, which I refused. I told him that I had already purchased one. "That is good," he said to me, and he gave me some tablets for the pain. As the month continued to run away, I had no choice but to start using my right hand for the first time to lift and carry heavy trays. It was kind of awkward, but I had no other choice but to use my right arm. My left wrist was still killing me, and I now realized that my right arm could not keep up with the pressure. My muscles around my right elbow started to feel sore, so I went back to see the ship's doctor in January 1996, and all he gave me was some more tablets. He then wrote on the remark form, which I had one copy of for myself, "Return if further problem," then he signed at the bottom of the form. An appointment was made several times for me to see a rheumatologist between January and February 1996. On the medical referral, it stated that it was tenosynovitis in the left wrist and requested to evaluate and treat it. On another occasion, the diagnosis was that my left wrist was strained, and I had no relief of Voltareen. I had come to the realization that the company doctors were trying to link arthritis to my injury that occurred on board.

The worse was yet to come: an appointment to see him in March 1996. Because the injection I received in my left wrist did not solve the problem, the ship's doctor filled out a crew shore side medical referral and signed his name to it. I made sure to keep one copy of this form, so everything was set. A day before my appointment, I received a vacation form to sign that meant that the following day when we docked in the United States port I had to leave the ship as a sick crew member. The following morning after finishing serving my last breakfast in pain, I paid one dining room cleaner to reset my station for dinner because I needed the extra time to surrender my life jacket at the bridge also to turn in my bed linen and uniform. I received my return ticket and a letter to return back to work within four months. How could I have fallen for a foolish move like this? The chances were like this because it really happened. There were crew members that received letters from the company stating that there were no spaces available at this time and they would be contacted. Some crew members ended up taking a permanent vacation. Some crew members were told to keep on calling in and checking to see if there was any space. I spoke to one of my ship colleagues about my work condition, and he told me to see a lawyer immediately after signing off the vessel. It was a fact that I met a lot of nice passengers who invited me to spend time with them whenever I was off the ship. Since I had no one to turn to, I had no choice but to call a good friend of mine and to remind him of the invitation he gave me. After explaining the situation that I found myself in, I was asked to stop by. So I rented a car for four days and drove down to this certain address where I was welcomed to the home of my friend. I made a lot of calls to various lawyers out of the phone book. Everyone I called that day told me that they did not take any seamen's cases. They were perfectly right because they knew that they were not good enough to go up against a multimillionaire lawyer. I believed they were looking for a much easier case to deal with.

I now remembered that I had two phone numbers in my wallet that I was given by two different crew members. These two lawyers were hundreds of miles from each other, and they both accepted my case. A great feeling came over me that day when these two lawyers told me the same thing and what I was entitled to and what role the company should have played toward me. It was their responsibility to provide for me a place to stay and to make sure that I had received proper medical attention until my knee, wrist, and elbow were healed plus my salary. None of the above was considered to be done. Respectfully I set an appointment with one of the lawyers and handed him all documents to prove that I was sick and was on treatment, plus my appointment document to prove that this was negligent. My lawyer asked me if I had a place to stay in the state. "Yes," I answered, "with a good friend."

He said, "I will try and set up an appointment with a specialist for you." As my memory served me right, he never asked me if my stay in the country needed to be extended or not. While staying at this certain address in Florida, I remember giving my lawyer every bit of information on how to contact me before I left his office. He told me that he would try to find a specialist close to where I was staying. Because he gave me the assurance that he had my case in his hands, I was hoping that he would at least call me. If there was even once when the phone rang and it was his voice, certainly I would have felt a little better for me to know what is the true possession. It was I who always made the call to him. Each time I called my lawyer and asked the secretary if he had gotten through with the doctor that he had been searching for, the answer was that they couldn't seem to locate one close to where I was staying. Now that my stay in the States was coming to an end, I had no choice but to call the airport and make my reservation. My destination was home sweet home. Luckily at the time, I only had one piece of luggage, and I had to pay the trolley man to push it to the line due to my illness. To lift my luggage to the scale was very painful.

I finally reached home with the hope that my case against the company that I once worked for would cause them to at least pay up, which was my constitutional right. Regardless of my health, my family was more than happy to see me. Immediately I tried to lift my one-year-old son for a hug and a kiss, but painfully I had to put him down. My family became very worried and said, "You must see a doctor soon."

I answered, "Yes, I will."

I knew a friend of the family who was a doctor. I happened to drive over twenty miles to see him for one reason only: for him to recommend a good specialist who could help me. After explaining this to him, he replied, "Yes, I can. There is one I know of in your hometown."

"Thank goodness," I said to him. "That would be much easier. Thank you for your help." I shook his hand and left. My brother-in-law was driving, and I hated the late-night driving. The following morning, my wife called in and made an appointment for me to see the doctor. I happened to visit the same doctor twice, and the medication I received from him did not seem to help me, just like those I received from the rheumatologist consultant in the States. Since my first home doctor's professional skills did not solve my problem, he had to refer me to another rheumatologist consultant for further research. My second doctor now examined me and put me on a different type of medication. I now started to feel the pressure because all the expenses were being paid from my pocket. I knew that I was unable to work, and it was impossible for me to be employed with my health condition. The first letter I received from my second doctor was faxed to my lawyer in the States. After a period of time, I decided to call my lawyer for a brief on the case. He told me that he had heard from the insurance company. He read the letter to me over the phone where the insurance company stated that I was no longer working with the company. I was the unlucky guy, for this statement was drawn against me. I was the unlucky guy who never received a letter or a phone call from my lawyer, not even once, for one full year. On many occasions, I would call his office, and the secretary would tell me to call him back. Each time that I called him back, he was still busy. I was told many times by the secretary that my lawyer would call me back. For one full year, I was left in the dark before I was told the status of the case at a minimum.

Chapter-36

Sports have been around for centuries and held the whole world at ransom, in which men became prisoners to this marvelous event and allowed their emotions to control them for life. Athletes become heroes in their own time and hold millions of fans in a chain of spectators. Not every man was born with the natural talent to become an athlete, but still they take sports seriously at all costs.

Most of the crew on board the ship respectfully believed that it was their constitutional right to participate in any sporting event at a risk one dared to take. Whether it was roller skating on shore while one was off duty, jogging to keep in shape, swimming at the beach, horseback riding, motorcycle riding, playing soccer or cricket, all these events were at one's own risk. I had seen the real purpose for sports between the crew members, especially when two ships from the same company docked together on an island: Once in a while or when we played against a different cruise line, this togetherness created new friends and caused us to believe that even though we worked for different cruise lines we saw ourselves as one big family. I found myself becoming a conspicuous person in the concept that in any event the conflict between some crew members would drastically give way to unity, but because sports is twofold, one can only hope that in the future man will continue to use sports as an instrument of God and peace. Because sports is twofold, it does not only portray friendliness on the playing field but implements evil thoughts within oneself, causing them to become treacherous against human dignity. It is a risk we as crew members took when two different departments on board decided to compete against each other or another company. In case of a serious accident on shore, we were not covered by any other insurance but our own if we had it. Outdoor entertainment was one of many ways a crew member sought to enjoy himself. Such as indoor, whether it is two music set playing against each other for the glory of being the number one sound on board the ship or other crew who believe in fighting. The impression I got was that if everyone on board was a karate expert, some definitely claimed that they were a black belt.

I remember one Pacific ship that I was working on was designed with car decks. These vehicles easily drove on and off, only in some ports. Whether the deck was fully loaded or not, there was always space for the masters of martial arts to compete. An event like this one definitely stayed beyond the knowledge of the management on board, and not all the crew members would know about this event. The problem normally started upstairs and ended up down on the car deck with no other physical weapons involved or any kind of betting, just a couple of crew members taking out their frustration on each other, which was forbidden by any company rules. Table tennis and basketball were common games played between the crew members. The crew members had to find something to do or else one could become a psychopath. What could we do to amuse ourselves? I had to make a choice for myself, and so did the other crew members. We disregarded any invitation we received from any management member because none of the above activities were mentioned on our contract. Speaking of my department only, it was a reality that other crew members and myself had to live with as long as we continued to sail upon the ocean or rage. There was always a dining room team leaving the ship after every lunch was finished in a certain port, where they would have one special driver that the team would use each cruise to transport them back and forth. This team dedicated themselves to pleasing the dining room management on board for more than one reason. Whether it was playing tennis or soccer, there were crew members who always wanted to be on such a team.

In any event that anyone chose to participate in, physical conflict normally was engaged with carelessness and caused physical injury. The ship's doctor would attend to anyone who claimed that they were ill, but where suing the company was concerned, it was out of the question. It was a pleasure to admire a full team walking off the gangway fully geared up with all kinds of equipment including food and first aid like soldiers who were ready for the battlefield. Not only the crew from the ship presented themselves as spectators but natives too. Whether they were not working or on a day off from work or at lunch break, the moment seemed fitting. This weekly practice by the crew also helped to advertise and professionally promote the company we worked for because it was our pride whenever we conversed with the natives to tell them how wonderful it was to cruise with us and how much they would enjoy their money's worth. During every cruise at least twenty crew members out of five hundred would promote the cruise line, still we were not recognized at certain points.

Now, back on board there was a big difference between the team who played from the non-players, especially when two dining rooms competed against each other because the dining room management fell in love with his special team. There was a possibility for the team to become his idol and constantly receive better treatment than other dining room personnel. What I have recognized for myself within the team was that one might get carried away when he truly recognized how much of an idol he had become to the management on board, and out of nowhere without knowing it, the standard regard for the department head started to deteriorate. The kind of chance this team would take with their job, a non-player did not dare to run such a risk.

On port days, the vessel was not completely empty of crew members who were off duty. Some crew members naturally dedicated their spare time to pumping iron and doing other workouts in the crew gym that was provided for them, but things did not always go well between them, and this mostly happened when the gym was overcrowded. Some crew members definitely had limited time to spare and needed to get in and out. Some crew members could not care less who was waiting, because they had a certain time that they would like to spend on each instrument. Each time a crew member finished using a piece of equipment, that individual was supposed to dry away the sweat from the support they used, whether it was sitting or lying down. Other crew members had to dry up sweat before using the equipment, and this kind of disregard to other fellow crew members certainly caused them to dislike each other. The next problem that easily caused hand-to-hand combat was the type of music one chose to play when one was working out. Music could get into one's head and create a bad mood and cause him to stop his training immediately. One could find another's music to be disturbing, which could be because it was too loud or if each crew member was listening to his own sound system or especially if the music's language was not in English.

There was a certain group amongst us crew members who spent their days off going deep-sea fishing. Most of us on board preferred the fresh catch that these guys brought for us. To make back their money that they used to rent the fishing boat, they would sell us their fresh catch of the day, and everyone would be eating fish for dinner. Since fishing was the only sport these guys found their pleasure in, every cruise that we docked in the Bahamas they would go fishing. For bait they would use squid that they purchased in the fish market. After a long period of time, death came knocking at their door. As I remember, this was their biggest catch of the year. Amongst their last catch was a large grouper fish weighing over fifty pounds. The fishing team would keep this one for themselves. This fish was brought to the pantry, which was the cold food preparation area in the kitchen, for the cooks to decorate it for picture taking. Since none of us were cooks, we paid the regular cooks for doing so. This was the biggest fish dinner ever held inside the ship's restaurant. The fishing team chose to sit by themselves with this large grouper properly cooked and laid in the center of their table. They alone could not devour such a massive portion, so a few of their close friends did partake of the dish. The liver was eaten by the captain of the fishing team. This was the happiest moment that ever surrounded the dining room team for a long time. This was a moment in time that no man who shared the same experience could ever forget. This was a mournful cry for everyone who participated in the fish-eating celebration. Most guys started to feel sick before midnight, and the captain of the fishing team who partook of the liver was most seriously poisoned. The doctor on board the vessel at that time had done a very excellent job by attending to the crew promptly with medical care. The individual who partook of the liver was in the ship's hospital for over three weeks, and after one month had passed, we the dining room team was happy to see him recovered although he was still looking sick. The management on board came up with new rules and regulations that no fish from shore side should be brought on board by the crew and no cook should be caught cooking in the main kitchen with fish caught from the outside because this was a food preparation area for passengers and strictly against the United States public health department.

About The Author

From wood and water, a little island no more than 4411 square miles called Jamaica and surrounded by the Caribbean Sea. A young man became a seaman in the early eighties where he worked amongst twenty-five different nationalities.

As a seaman He has sailed to more than twenty-five different ports half way across the globe.

The Pacific Ocean, the Caribbean Sea - east and west, Gulf of Mexico, Quebec to New, and Vancouver to Alaska.

As a waiter from the island, it was very difficult for him to get a position as a dining room waiter, as they use more Europeans. The opportunity of equal earning was lacking. He was tempted to do drugs, he was tempted to do stow away. In which he had done none of the above.

Printed in the United States
30911LVS00001B/76-255